Rose's Tale

The Strap, the Wooden Compass – The Endless Abuse at School

By Gaynor Jones

Published by Pen It! Publications, LLC in the U.S.A.
812-371-4128 www.penitpublications.com

ISBN: 978-1-954004-88-7
Edited by: April Hale Maguire

During the course of publishing this book, Gaynor's mother, Rose, passed away peacefully on June 14, 2020. She will always be remembered with much love.

Y. N. W. A.

INTRODUCTION

I am dedicating this story to my mum, Rose. You will read about how she grew up in post-war England, with only a single mum left to raise her and her seven siblings after her father died.

She received constant abuse from her teachers at school, which is not tolerated in today's society. I want to bring to light this abuse, so others can know about it. This was an era when there was no child protection. The treatment to Rose was not only endured by her, but also many other children suffered the same abuse.

Her story takes place in the 1940s and 1950's England in a city called St. Helen's, County of Lancashire, England. St. Helen's is the midway point between Manchester and Liverpool. This is where she lived until she married.

I am here to tell her story of the mental and physical abuse she suffered at the hands of her teachers whom she should have been able to trust. They should have praised her for her accomplishments and comforted her when she was down and scared. This was not to be, in Rose's school life. Children knew to never talk back to an adult. There was a definite distinction between the two classes of children.

My name is Gaynor, and I am Rose's eldest daughter. I am telling her story in her words. The story is based on her memories, thoughts, words, and feelings. She often tells me how they treated her during her school years. It was so unnecessary.

She is speaking out now for all the children that went through the same things she endured. She is their voice. Child labour laws never existed back then. Nothing was ever done about the abuse. This will show and tell you how the British teachers treated children back in those days.

My mum, Rose, is now 76. I am grateful for her input in writing this story about her. Some of the memories she has forgotten, names, dates, etc., because it has been so long, but I want to talk about what she does remember. She still remembers how she was treated and those who abused her. That never went away. To

this day, my mother does not know how to swim, so she never got the opportunity to learn.
She is very afraid of the water to this day, and if she goes in it, she is only up to her shoulders. This incident has affected her entire life.

If someone wants to take advantage of her or she thinks they are, she gets very defensive and on guard. She doesn't make friends easily and is guarded.

If anyone does anything bad to her, she pretty much writes them off and never speaks to them again. Here is another example of what I am talking about. This is how it has life-long effects on her.

We had a garage sale this summer and were selling my dad's tools after his passing. Mom wanted it, but she got very angry and aggressive during the sale. She had "looks could kill" kind of eyes. I had never seen my mom act like that before. It worried me a great deal. I explained to her that she wanted the sale, it had to be gone, and nobody was stealing dad's stuff. They were buying it. Mom was acting like a four-year-old that day, having a temper tantrum. I have never seen her like that. I understood that these tools were my dad's world; and she felt like she was getting rid of him and everything that mattered to him.

My sister and I tried to explain that they were only material things, he would have been glad to know someone else was doing something with them.

It seems back in those days; the teachers did what they wanted and didn't care how it would affect the students. Why should they have been caned or strapped just because they couldn't spell? Why was it that their clothes weren't brand new and pretty? It was so wrong. I am glad to see a child's rights are finally being taken seriously, but it still angers me to see children abused.

Therefore, I am writing "Rose's Tale," to show others to never treat children the way she and others were treated. Children are there for you to love, nurture and protect them, not to abuse them.

Thank you, Mom. You are such a strong lady having to relive this again for me.

I am telling Mum's story and her home life. She provided the information, so I am telling her part in this. This is how Mum told me her story.

While asking mom for this information, whether it be over the phone or face to face at her kitchen table over a cup of tea and coffee, mom never cried once. She laughed at some of the events, but was very positive and open about all she endured.

Table of Contents

ROSE

The date was May 26, 1943. A baby girl was born. She was the sixth child of Robert and Louisa Arnold. They named her Rose. All births in those years were home births. Unless there was a problem that could involve the mum or baby, a hospital was never used. You had a doctor and a midwife with you.

Rose was born while England was in the midst of the Second World War. She met her siblings, Elsie, Mary, Vera, Billy, and Ellen. The family later welcomed Jean and Brenda to the Arnold household. Rose was born in St. Helen's, Merseyside UK. St. Helens was known for its two major companies Beecham Pharmaceuticals and Pilkington Glass. St. Helens township was established in 1868. Other big employers were the coal and copper mines for smelting.

Louisa Arnold (nee Hollihead) was the family matriarch, Rose's mother. She is approximately 4 feet 7 inches tall, with blue eyes, and curly white hair that comes to her shoulders, and she was chubby. Her hair turned completely white when she turned forty.

Louisa always wore a flowered dress of some print, a pinafore over her dress, and she wore bloomers. She always had on knee-high stockings and either a pair of slip-on shoes or her slippers.

Robert, Rose's dad worked in Liverpool as a gardener for Lord Stanley. The estate he worked at was known as Knowsley Safari Park. There was the main family home surrounded by 2500 acres of parkland, which contained the Safari Park. It still is a fully functioning safari park to this day, and they welcome thousands of visitors a year to the park. The stately home is used for events, weddings etc. Robert rode the bus to work. No one could afford a car in those days, and it was too far for him to walk.

Liverpool was about four miles from home. Lord Stanley donated a cup to the National Hockey League which is what we know today to be the Stanley Cup. It was donated by Governor General Lord Stanley in 1892 for presentation to the top hockey team in Canada and was first awarded to the Montreal Amateur Athletic Association (1892–93).

Rose's dad worked for Lord Stanley until he was no longer able to work. He was in his late sixties when he died, leaving Louisa to raise the children all alone. Rose was only four years old when her dad passed away. They lived in a two-story council house. There were happy times for the family, and some not so happy times but they survived. Each family member looked out for the other. They were poor but happy. Louisa relied on a widow's pension, ration books and financial help from the government to care for her family.

Food was scarce after the war, and everyone had to ration. Each family had a ration book from the government. The ration book consisted of stamps for food and clothing Louisa could get for the family. Each family member had their own ration book, so they had eight books altogether. Each stamp had perforated edges and an item of food or clothing listed on it.

At the beginning of the Second World War in 1939, the United Kingdom was importing 20,000,000 long tons of food per year, including about 70% of its cheese and sugar, nearly 80% of fruits and about 70% of cereals and fats. The UK also imported more than half of its meat and relied on imported feed to support its domestic meat production. The civilian population of the country was about 50 million. To attack shipping bound for Britain was one of the principal strategies of the Germans in the Battle of the Atlantic, restricting British industry and potentially starving the nation into submission.

To deal with extreme shortages at times, the Ministry of Food instituted a system of rationing. To buy most rationed items, each person had to register at chosen shops and was provided with a ration book containing coupons. The shopkeeper was provided with enough food for registered customers. Purchasers had to take ration books with them when shopping so that the relevant coupon or coupons could be canceled.

On 8 January 1940, bacon, butter, and sugar were rationed. This was followed by successive ration schemes for meat, tea, jam, biscuits, breakfast cereals, cheese, eggs, lard, milk, and canned and dried fruit. Fish was not rationed, but prices increased considerably as the war progressed. Rose's family was never able to enjoy fish since they couldn't afford to buy it.

Most controversial was bread; it was not rationed until after the war ended, but the "national loaf allotted to all" was made of whole meal bread which replaced the ordinary white variety. To the distaste of most housewives, they found it mushy, grey, and easy to blame for digestion problems. Clothing was rationed on a points system. The family relied on hand me downs and donations.

(See this reference for more information on rationing)
https://en.wikipedia.org/wiki/Rationing_in_the_United_Kingdom

Each stamp allowed one person to have one piece of candy or one pound of butter per week. Louisa realized that there wouldn't be enough stamps; so, she decided to swap some of them. She traded them with other ladies, for the items she needed; and vice versa. She often traded in her candy stamps for extra margarine for the children. She couldn't afford butter, so she got margarine instead. This was how everyone survived until England could get back on its feet. Even with these stamps, the food amounts were never enough for a family this size.

One loaf of bread had to feed nine of us, the same with everything else. Food didn't go far. From time to time, Mum sent us to the local Red Cross to get a hot meal there.

A typical meal consisted of a bowl of "scouse" for everyone. Scouse was the Liverpool version of what we know to be stew. Sometimes we were able to have a slice of bread, but rarely as one loaf did not go far to feed a big family.

The UK government gave orders that every person in the UK, because of the war and citizens being malnourished, were to be given a daily teaspoon of cod liver oil, followed by a glass of orange juice and one small bottle of milk. If someone refused to take the cod liver oil, they were not allowed to have the orange juice and the bottle of milk. This got us through the bad times.

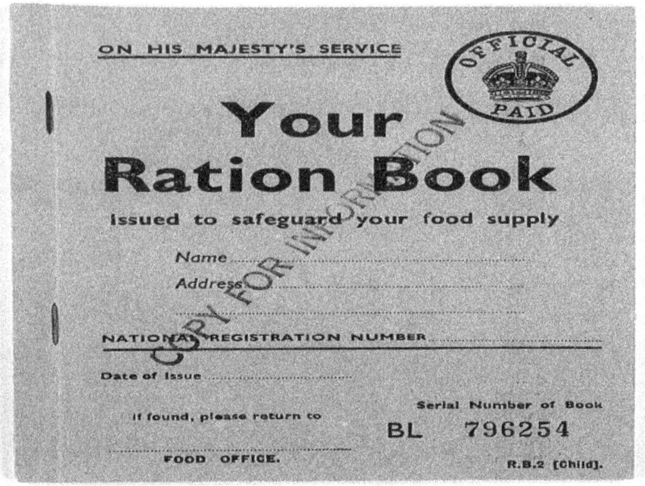
ON HIS MAJESTY'S SERVICE

OFFICIAL PAID

Your
Ration Book

issued to safeguard your food supply

Name ....

Address ....

NATIONAL REGISTRATION NUMBER ....

Date of Issue ....

If found, please return to

FOOD OFFICE.

Serial Number of Book

BL 796254

R.B.2 [Child].

COPY FOR INFORMATION

This is what a ration book looked like. Each person got one.

HERE MY STORY BEGINS

as told by Rose to me

Chapter 1
My Background

I grew up with my parents Louisa and Robert in a two-story council house in St. Helen's. We live in a suburb called Portico. Our style of house is called a council house. There are a lot of them. The houses are on a huge council estate. Our house is a two-story brown brick home with a slate roof, it had three bedrooms. I can best describe them as a semi. All of the bedrooms are on the second floor. There is a very large three-paned window at the front of the house which is where the living room is located.

On the second floor is another three-paned window. Approximately three-quarters of our property is surrounded by a reddish coloured wooden fence. The sidewalk is near the fence. There is a gate which can be opened to the pathway that leads to the front door; and the side of the house. There is a small piece of grass in the front yard; our backyard is open to the backyards of all the houses in that particular area. None of us have fenced in backyards; it is a big open grassed field. We spend hours playing football there, and cricket, along with skipping rope. Our parents, and we kids, know we are pretty safe playing back there because everyone could see us playing there.

Downstairs is the living room, kitchen, and bathing room. The bathing room has an emersion heater in it, to heat the water whenever we need it.

It takes about twenty minutes to heat up the water after you flip the switch. That is also the room where the bathtub is. It is your typical medium-sized bathroom. The walls are light blue with a white cast iron tub and a simple modest sink.

My living room is where we spend a lot of time. It is the gathering spot for us all. There is a three-piece settee (couch and chairs) in it. The furniture is covered in blue cotton. There are two matching armchairs that make the chesterfield a set. Mum has a china cabinet there which holds antiques passed down to her from her family. In front of the living room window, there is a table and a couple of chairs. This is where some of us eat when the kitchen table cannot hold us all. On top of our mantel, there is a radio. That's where we get our news or listen to music.

My sisters and I love nothing more than moving the chesterfield in the living room, to make an open spot in the middle of the floor, turn on the radio and dance around to the music. We pretend that we are at some fancy dance. We pull our dress bottoms sideways and twirl around to the music. I love American music, especially Elvis Presley.

The one thing I dislike the most about the house is the location of the toilet. It is in a separate room from the bath. As you come in the side door, you see to your left a small room with a door before you go into the house. Inside that room is a toilet. There is no heating in it. It is so cold in the winter you shiver.

The tank is way up high near the ceiling, with the toilet bowl on the floor level. The only source of light is a bulb with a chain that you pull to turn it on and off.

It is very cold in the winter, so you make very few trips to use it. The house is half of a semi. The coal shed is on the side of the house close to the door, so you don't have to go far to get more. It is a bricked hole with a door and handles to open it or close it. The coal is safe from the elements.

Every living room has a coal fireplace. This is the way you heat the home. There is no such thing these days as turning on a radiator or furnace for heating. We use the fireplace. It would get toasty warm, but you had to keep tending to the fire. Each time you needed wood or coal for it, someone would have to take a pail and go outside to the coal shed and fill it up.

It only heated the main floor of the house; the upstairs never got any heat. That is the way it is back in England in those years.

When we have been playing outside, we run inside, throw our shoes off and stand in front of the fire to warm up. It sure doesn't take long to get warm again and toasty dry.

Many homes use wallpaper as the main décor on the walls. You can see it in the living room or sitting room. In the living room it is cream coloured with periwinkle blue flowers all over it. The curtains are cream coloured. The house has three doors near the front door entrance.

One of the doors leads to the Lecce box room, there is another that when opened it leads to the living room. The third door leads to the upstairs living quarters. The walls going upstairs to the second floor also have wallpaper.

We cannot afford to own a television, but we do have a radio that we can keep up to date with about things that are going on in the world. We all sit around the radio after supper and listen to the news or play music. This is our only means of keeping up with what is going on with the war.

Our house has electricity and plumbing. By the front door, there is a cupboard style small room. Inside there is a box for the electricity. We refer to it as the lecce box You have to put in 5 pence for the electricity and have to do the same thing when the time runs out. It is a small pantry sized room with a chain pull light from the ceiling. You can imagine how much fun it is to find the box and turn the light on in the dark when the money has run out, and you have to re-feed the meter. Thank goodness for a candle or torch. On hooks next to the lecce box are our gas masks that the government has given us.

If a bomb were to drop, they tell us to grab the masks and run out to the back yard where there is a bomb shelter. We each have one in our homes, so there were eight in my house. There it is safe, and we can take shelter.

The government is more worried about us getting gassed, that is why they give us all a gas mask. The shelter we have to run to looks like a garden shed but is made of corrugated tin. We never have to go in there and use it. It is a cautionary building in case we ever have to use it.

The bombs are close, and I remember hearing them from inside our house. There is a siren that goes off when there is a bomb nearby. It is super loud. You cannot miss hearing the sound of it. When it sounds, there is a loud squeal one can hear for miles.

You have to run to the closet where the gas masks are, put them on, and then head for the shed at the bottom of the yard. You have to stay there until the sirens stop. I can hear the sirens go, I run into the house as fast as I can, grab my gas mask and run to the bomb shed. My whole family is doing the same thing. All I can hear is everyone in the area yelling, "The Gerries are coming, the Gerries are coming." It means that the Germans are flying overhead. You cannot imagine how scary that is.

Mum's kitchen is fair sized. She uses a gas stove to cook our meals. The walls are a light green. There are two good-sized windows in it, and they let in a lot of light. They overlook the backyard of the house. We have no fridge now. They are a luxury we cannot afford. In England, these days you don't freeze the meat. Shopping is usually done every other day for those of us who do not have a fridge.

On Saturday's we take our ration book and head up the road to the local co-op; which is three blocks from the house. We are all excited as it is a shopping day.

Mum hands her ration stamp book to the storekeeper and we bring home what we need and can get for Sundays meal. The women would often trade stamps depending on who needed what. Mum would often trade her candy stamps for extra bread or margarine for us.

We have a kitchen table with chairs, but it is not big enough for everyone to sit around. My older siblings usually end up eating in the living room. Tea is the main beverage we drink. My mum buys PG Tips. A pot of tea goes a long way so that is what we drink. Water as well. Juices are rare as the ships bringing them to England are often blown up by the Germans. Finally, there are eggs to buy. They come powdered in a tin can with an American eagle on the outside.

As I stated, there are three bedrooms upstairs. My brother Billy is the only boy in the home, so he has his own bedroom. The other bedroom at the end of the hall has a double bed in it. My older sisters Elsie and Ellen sleep there. They are older than me. Elsie is the eldest of the two. They live there until they wed.

My bed is in the big bedroom looking out over the front yard of the house. The bedroom is a large-sized room with two double beds in it. We have a dresser that we both share. The bedroom has a huge window facing the front yard and street that I can look out of. This bedroom also has two double beds in it. My other sisters Vera, Jean, and Brenda sleep in one bed. Jean and Brenda are only toddlers now, so all three fit in the bed.

I sleep in the other bed with my mum. We have no heating upstairs, so we count on our combined body heat and lots of blankets to keep us warm. We all have five blankets on our beds to sleep but we are still cold some days. It is the damp air that makes it colder. The coal fire doesn't stay lit all night either, so the house cools down.

No council houses have heating upstairs. My mum is on the chubby side, so I usually put my arms under her arms and that keeps me extra warm. I love this bedroom cuddling up to her. Thank goodness she doesn't snore; it never takes long for us to fall into a deep sleep.

I often stand looking out the large window in the bedroom and watch the rain and thunder during storms. I enjoy watching the people walking and the double-decker buses that pass by. There is nothing more peaceful than the sound of the rain hitting the roof and windows.

Mum is four and a half feet tall, chubby as I said. She has blue eyes, a heart-shaped face and curly white hair. Mum's hair is turning completely white at the age of 40. She is always wearing a dress, a pinafore (apron) and bloomers instead of panties. She also wears knee-high hose, or what we called nylons or knee-highs. She is always laughing and smiling which surprises me with all the tension we cause her.

I do not know how mum can stay so calm and tolerate all our problems as she does. She is a very strong woman who has a wicked sense of humour. We always make each other laugh. I also have an older sister Mary. She lives a block away from us and often drops by to visit. There are six girls living at home now. There is always some sort of drama happening. One jealous of the other, someone got something the others didn't. Mum is as fair as she can be.

Chapter 2
Weekends at the Arnold House

On Saturday we all spend our morning walking downtown to the local market. The name of it is the Tontine Market. It is always packed with people. I love walking down here, it's the highlight of my week.

We have to buy cups as we are breaking them, especially the younger children. It is a treat for us all. I run from stall to stall admiring all the goods for sale. I come up to a case full of cakes, pastries and I keep yelling, "I want this, I want that." My sisters pull me away, telling me I cannot have them. I pout but I listen to them.

The one thing we pick up is a Madeira cake; it is a treat for all. What is a Madeira cake, I'm sure you're wondering? A Madeira cake is a sponge cake. It appears to always be dry on the outside, but the inside is so moist. You can buy it either loaf-shaped or round shaped. Mum gives the older girls her list and they go and get any cups or dishes we need replacing.

We younger ones walk around with mum and admire whatever was there. We walk and it keeps us fit.

Depending on what Saturday it turns out to be, the church has a rummage sale. All of the neighbourhood mums show up to the sale and get clothing to wear.

Mum spends her time buying dresses, tops or shirts, cardigans (sweaters) and shoes. We cannot wait until she comes home with the clothes for us. They are new clothes and we try them on and model them in front of all the other sisters. She always makes sure she buys whatever fits us.

Shoes usually have holes in the bottom, I don't care. None of us care. They are new shoes to us. If they have holes in the soles, we know how to fix them, so they look new and nobody knows anything different. We put a piece of cardboard in the bottom of the shoe. It keeps them dry and our feet clean.

Saturday is also washing day around our house. You can imagine how many clothes mum has to wash with nine of us there. It is a chore. In the kitchen, there is a big boiler. We have to drop our clothes in it, in order for them to get clean. Everything is then hung out on the clothesline in the back yard. The clothes are stiff when they come back in, but boy do they smell good with the fresh air-drying them.

Sunday mum is baking all day. It is so much fun watching her bake. She is wearing her baking apron. She is rolling and kneading with flour all over her and the table while baking a rhubarb pie. Next, she is also making a coconut pie, followed by a jam pie and finally, a pound cake. These are going to be our desserts for the week, or so she hopes they will last the week. It never happens in our house.

We stand alongside mum while she is measuring, or rolling, whatever she needs doing. Every weekend is the same thing. Her baking is amazing.

All of my sisters and I are good bakers after learning from mum. I usually do the stirring because I haven't quite perfected the art of rolling yet. These are happy times for everyone. After baking it is time for us all to start making tea. The smell in the house is amazing. I cannot wait to taste it.

Each Sunday for tea consists of what meat mum can get. She always makes cabbage with it or potatoes.

Some Sundays it might be scouse, other ones it might be a rabbit. Other times we are having corned beef and hash. Cabbage goes far so mum usually cooks that.

I know you're wondering how long it takes us to eat those delicious pies she bakes. Well, I can tell you this, by Monday everything is gone. Nothing left. Monday nights are the worse. Our cupboards are bare. Tuesday morning mum gets her pension check, so we have a little bit of money again.

During the weekdays, mum usually makes us chips and eggs, or toast and beans, or chips and eggs, fish, and chips.

I love anything with chips; fish and chips, beans and toast, eggs, and beans. My favourite is a boiled egg with soldiers. It is a soft boiled egg with toast cut into strips. That is a soldier.

These items are never enough for us to feel full, but it puts something on our bellies before bedtime. We are still hungry so that is why we go to the school canteens for lunches.

Bath nights are Sundays. Remember earlier I had mentioned about an immersion heater. To have enough hot water for you to bathe in, mum has to flip on the immersion heater switch to heat up the water. It takes about twenty minutes for it to reach the right temperature. Water is not wasted during those years with the war, so we all got bathed in the same bathwater. It's like swamp water when the youngest sister Brenda gets her bath. We use lye soap which goes far enough for all us to have a bath. We always try to conserve as much water and electricity as we can.

Mum bathes us one by one until we are all clean, the eldest child to the youngest. After it, we can't wait to get wrapped up in our towels and run into the living room and stand in front of the coal fire to dry. My older sisters help out. I sure love that warm heat drying me off. I get toasty warm.

It is soon bedtime. Mum tells me it's time for bed so I run up the stairs, close the curtains and jump into bed. I fall to sleep quickly.

Chapter 3
Rose Begins School

I begin primary school in 1947. My school is St. Matthew's School. This is where my story begins with physical and mental abuse. I am about four and a half years old now. In a few days, I will be starting kindergarten. I am so happy and also excited. I am sad too that I will be away from my mum all day. I'm not used to that.

My first day of school is typical of how a child's day should be. I am nervous not knowing what school is all about and being away from my mum for the first time ever, I am scared. I wake up and get dressed in my usual clothes which is a dress with a cardigan over it. I always wear white socks with shoes, but they have holes in the soles of them. I don't have a hairbrush so I make it look as good as I can. Girls in those days never wore pants, but always wore a dress or skirt and blouse with a cardigan (sweater). My heart is pounding as I walk to school not knowing what to expect when I get there. Mum walks with me but I am feeling anxious and sick to my stomach.

I arrive at St. Matthews and go running to the playground where all the other kids are playing. Mum kisses me goodbye in the playground and I am crying so many tears.

She won't show it but she tells me later that day that she cried all the way home too. The school headmistress comes outside with a huge bell in one hand, and rings it to tell us that it is time to begin school.

She is in her sixties and well dressed. She is busy getting everything in order but seems like a very nice lady. Our teacher leads us to our classroom. You can feel the excitement from everyone.

The headmistress is very liked by the older students, so I know she will be nice. She makes me feel very much at ease. Her name is Mrs. Livingstone. A headmistress is what we know as a Principal in North America. The school was established in 1867 and it closed in 2004. Each classroom from Kindergarten to Grade Four is the primary section. From Grade Five to Eight is the senior section. We have approximately twenty- three students in each grade.

Kindergarten and Grade One go by without incident for me. I am a happy-go- lucky, care-free child and eager to learn what the world has to teach me. I love coloring and find nap time is the best.

Kindergarten is fun; we play with toys. Supplies like paint and crayons are not available due to the war. A lot of supplies are being destroyed by the Germans who have torpedoed the supply ships or blown them up. These things you cannot get for schools. We do not have instruments either for music class, so we sing instead.

Morning play times are milk times and we have a third of a pint daily with thirty little bottles to a crate. There is no playground equipment or climbing apparatus, but we take rubber balls and rope outside with us to play with. We make our own fun with what little we have to play with. I love skipping and playing hopscotch, and I am a bit of a tomboy so I love to run around the playground.

The bell rings after our morning classes so I make my way to the school canteen for a hot lunch. Children that are poor are able to go to this canteen so we can at least have one hot, nutritious meal. They insist on that. The food isn't that great but I eat it. I run home as fast as I can before the lunch period is over to see mum, then run back to school for the afternoon classes.

After school, I head outside to play with the neighborhood kids. My favorite activity is skipping. I skip until the gas lamps are lit; by then it is time to head inside and get ready for bed. They are gas lamps that are lit in the evening and put out in the morning. A man comes on his bicycle with a large ladder in tow. He climbs his ladder up to the lamp and fills it with some type of illuminating gas-liquid. He then proceeds to light it. In the morning, the same thing happens; he shows up but puts it out this time.

Grade One begins. My teachers' name is Mrs. Johnson who I am very fond of. She is a tall woman, long dark hair which she always wears up in a bun. She is around fifty to fifty-two years of age. She always wears a dress to class and is very kind and helpful to the students. She also teaches sewing to older grade students. I do very well in Grade One. I also have a lot of friends.

I have survived my first day. I had so much fun. I cannot wait to go back another day. As soon as I get home, I can't wait to open the door and tell my mum all about how my day was. Mum sits me down on the settee (couch) and wants to hear all about it. I am talking so fast I don't know how she hears anything I said. If she doesn't hear it all, she sure never shows me.

Grade One goes by uneventful. We learn the usual reading, writing, arithmetic. I love reading. It is my favourite subject. I can take myself to different countries, or situations through the book I'm reading. Reading is over, now it is time to move on to arithmetic.

This is not my favourite subject but I have to learn it. There goes the bell. It's recess time. I can't wait to go outside. I always look forward to this part of the day.

We have a school nurse and each day she comes into the classes to do a head-lice check. She makes sure that everyone is lice free, and the class is not full of them. When any of us see the nurse coming, we always say, "Oh there's Nitty Nora the bug explorer."

A nit is an English name for head lice. I get my usual cuts and bumps but no serious injuries at school.
In the mornings we have our usual third of a pint of milk. For lunch, I head to the local canteen and have lunch there. There are a few minutes left before we have to head back to class for the afternoon. I run home and see my mum. She loves having me home for those few minutes. I then run back to school.

During the summer term, I spend as much time as I can outdoors playing with my friends and the neighborhood kids. We are usually outside from dawn until dinner. After dinner, I do my homework if there is homework. If not, I am outside playing until bedtime.

My friends and I are rarely at home. We are much happier being outside in the fresh air than being indoors. One favourite park to go to is Taylor Park. I love playing on the swings there, splashing in the water. There is a big lake in the middle of the park and paddle boats that people can use.

Chapter 4
Grade 2 the Abuse Begins

Grade Two is when I begin to endure ridicule and physical abuse from my teachers. The first one is a teacher called Mrs. Taylor. I have this terrible feeling coming over me. The feeling that something is not good, something is going to happen, and it doesn't feel right. I cannot shake it.

Upon entering the classroom, I can see Mrs. Taylor staring at me. Her eyes are glaring right at me and through me. Her nose wrinkles up as if she is disgusted. Her eyebrows and nose scrunch up as if to say, "Who is this child, and what is she wearing? How could a child come to school looking like this?" I know deep down what she is thinking as I make my way to my desk to prepare for the day ahead. I don't know what to think of her at that moment, and I have this feeling that it is not good. My feelings are completely right.

After that look, I get a sick feeling not wanting to go to school again. Knowing what I have to face from this teacher when I get there. It takes every ounce of energy in me to go into the classroom. My heart is racing like butterflies. I'm nauseous, like I want to turn around and run home.

My heart is going to jump out of my chest. I make my way to my desk, hoping she won't see me. I don't feel any different from any of the other girls. I even have on a new dress.

Class is the same as Grade One except the information is getting a little harder. I am excited to be learning my ABC's and how to count.

My class is getting prepared for Harvest time. It is like Thanksgiving to others. Each student has to bring in a vegetable to contribute to it. My mum cannot afford expensive vegetables or afford to buy extra vegetables for each of us to take in. She makes sure though we have something to give. Mum buys one bag of potatoes and gives each of us a potato to take in.

I hand in my one potato, feeling so proud I brought in something to share for the harvest. I hand it in, and as soon as I do, I immediately see the scowl from the teacher. I hurry to my desk, walking as fast as I can. I am very tense.

Mrs. Taylor's voice starts to get loud so everyone can hear her. She points out to the class who brought in what and proudly praises the students whose parents have a good living. I hear, "Rose, come to the front of the class." So, I go. I am now standing in front of the class and she goes to find one of the more privileged kids. She usually picks Lucy to stand beside me. Lucy is about an inch taller than I am with blonde hair and brown eyes and she is also well dressed. I am dressed in my hand me downs.

I can see her finger extend out my way, point to the vegetables and say, "Oh look how Lucy's mom sent her with a beautiful large cauliflower or a big green cabbage." Then she turns her gaze towards me and says, "Now look at Rose. What did Rose bring in? One potato. Now, Lucy's mom loves her. She is always dressed in the finest clothes with ribbons in her hair and her shoes are polished. Now, here's Rose. Her mum is a terrible mum who can't clothe or feed her."

She seems quite proud insulting me like that. I am humiliated in front of everyone. She does not care. I am always on my best behavior and try to please her, but nothing I do matters.

I want to cry but I will never give her or the other students the satisfaction of letting them know how much it hurts me. The words and her actions cut into me like a knife. I never feel worthless or poor at home, but this teacher sure likes to make me feel that way in class. She gets some kind of personal satisfaction out of it and the feeling of superiority over me.

Why would anyone get pleasure out of doing this to a child? Her words played in my mind the rest of the day. On the walk home from school I have a little cry, and then wipe the tears from my face so it doesn't appear that I have been crying.

I do not want to show how sad I am, and I cannot tell me mum anything about it. There is no reason why I want her to feel bad that she cannot provide more for all. I never want her to feel that she is not a good mother, or feel responsible and guilty that she cannot provide more for us. She is doing the best she can and

I'm grateful for that. Mrs. Taylor doesn't know my mum; she's a Meany and a snob. My mother is a funny, kind lady.

All the food that we hand in at school is donated to the local hospitals to be used for the patients' meals. Ours is sent to Whiston Hospital where I am going to shortly be a patient for an illness I am soon to come down with. I get through Harvest time and continue with my studies. Soon it will be Christmas time.

I am hoping Christmas time will be better. I am looking forward to all the activities we are doing for Christmas. It is time for making decorations, singing, and doing fun things. Things will be different this time, not like Harvest time. I keep thinking that way. My hopes get crushed like a walnut in a nutcracker.

Each student has to bring in a square of jelly, a bit of sugar in brown paper, and a little bit of flour to make cookies. Jelly in England is not the same as we know it. It is more like Jell-O.

I am able to join in making paper chains to decorate the classroom for the Christmas party. I am surprised she is letting me take part in the festivities. I swallow my pride and take part as much as I can in the Christmas activities. Who can I complain to? There was absolutely no one. The teachers do what they want without a thought of what it does to their victim.

Mrs. Taylor not only abuses me in the classroom, she also abuses me in the school lunch canteen. There are free lunch meals given to those less fortunate and I am one of them having the meal. The meals consist of fish and chips, scouse (stew) or some kind of meat and vegetables. I look down at the plate of food in front of me and to my horror, there is boiled celery as the vegetable. I start feeling nauseous. I eat one bit and it is the most horrible, disgusting thing that anyone would want to eat. I finish the rest of the food on my plate but I cannot bring myself to eat the celery.

While eating, I see Mrs. Taylor coming towards me and she then stands right behind me. She can see that I am not eating the boiled celery. I am thinking oh no, what is she going to do to me? She reaches out her arm in front of her and she starts to pull on my ear. She then asks me, “Don’t you want it?” I said to her that I have tried to eat it, but I do not like boiled celery.

My stomach is churning from the taste and consistency of it. Can you imagine eating it boiled? I gulp it down; breathing through my nose so I don't have to taste it. It is horrible. I force myself to eat it. She starts to tell me that I am lucky to have a hot meal. If I was at home I would be starving. "It's free, eat it."

She tells me again that "my mum is not a good mum because she can't afford to feed us all." I want to scream and yell at her to leave me alone. How dare she say the things she does to any child? I don't understand. I am looking forward to Christmas break so I don't have to go to school then, and I can get away from her.

Christmas holidays are happy times. We make the best out of Christmas that we can. We are all together, and that is all that matters to me. You don't need expensive presents; family time is all one needs. It is Christmas Eve and Father Christmas will be coming soon. I rush to my bed to be asleep when he comes. I leave a sock at the edge of my bed for him. I have a hard time falling asleep because I am so excited, but I do.

Some of our decorations are handmade. We go on scavenger hunts around the estate and pick up acorn shells and bits of greenery. Whatever we can find to make into decorations, we make. If we find coloured paper, we make paper chains and other decorations. I love making decorations with acorns. I also love to cut out paper snowflakes and hang them from the ceiling and door frames.

My friends and I like to go out Christmas caroling in the evenings and weekends. We hang holly and ivy up around the door jams. Holly and ivy are an important part of Christmas decorations here in England.

I wake up early Christmas morning and can't wait to see what Father Christmas has left in my sock. He has left me one candy, one apple, and a chocolate bar. You know what? I love the chocolate bar.

I am thrilled to get it. It is a much-loved treat I only get at Christmas time. There is never any money for toys. I never get a toy to play with Christmas morning. I do get a colouring book that is already coloured in and broken crayons.

I get to colour, that's all I care about. I am so grateful. I spend hours colouring in my book. I tell mum that I want to help her with our Christmas dinner, so she lets me. I peel the potatoes, prepare the vegetable, and she is in charge of the chicken. I am excited for the roast chicken we are having. I do hide my chocolate bar from my sisters or I know they will eat it all.

The rest of the year is learning in class with the usual abuse from Mrs. Taylor. I plug away and do the best I can. It is February. Time for Shrove Tuesday. Mum makes us all pancakes for supper. We top them off with sugar and lemon juice. Everyone's belly is full after this dinner.

It is this year His Royal Highness King George VI dies. Out of respect for him, we all have a certain regimen we follow when a monarch dies. Our radios have news on but instead of the usual music we listen to, it is all somber music.

It could be best described as funeral music if I had to describe it. Those that can afford to own a television turn it off until after his funeral.

We all cover our windows with a black sheet or curtain. Whatever pictures we have on the wall are all turned backward, so we don't show vanity. It might sound crazy to those reading it, but that is what happens, and expected when a Monarch dies. The mourning period lasts twelve days. Princess Elizabeth returns from her tour and preparations are underway for her Coronation the following year.

The funeral is over and lives go back to normal. Easter comes and goes. It's winding down to the end of school year.

School is over; I can have fun outside playing again. I am so glad to get away from Mrs. Taylor. I never have to have her as my teacher again. She is a horrible, mean teacher. I cannot get home fast enough to my safety and sanctuary, my home.

Chapter 5
My Hospitalization

During the summer break this year I get very sick. I am losing a lot of weight. I am sick often; a rash has developed and I have a stiff neck. Mum is very worried so she goes down the road to call the doctor. The doctors make home visits, so he comes to the house to see me.

He arrives and I see that he is a tall, dark-haired man in his fifties. He rides his bike to see his patients, carrying his medical bag in one hand. He knocks on the front door and mum lets him in. I am lying on the couch with a blanket covering me, and he comes over to check me out to see what is wrong. He concludes that I am suffering from meningitis. I have all the classic symptoms. I need to get to the hospital as soon as possible.

There are no such things as house phones. The doctor gets on his bike and rides to the phone booth down the road and calls for an ambulance for me. He dials 999. The medics show up and I am taken by ambulance to Whiston Hospital for treatment.

They treat me by putting me under sun-ray lamps. They say that I need this. I want my mum with me but they won't allow that. I start crying, my body tremoring, I am begging and pleading for my mum to come in the room with me.

Of course, the hospital won't let this happen. I gather up every ounce of courage I have and face what I have to do by myself.

I am pushed on a bed down the hall to the room, and I catch a glance of my mum sobbing. In that room, I get stripped naked. I have to lie on the hospital bed and am given special goggles to protect my eyes. I have to lie under this lamp each day for thirty minutes. I have never felt so scared or so alone. My heart is pounding, and my body is trembling. After thirty minutes, I am taken back to my room where my mum is waiting for me. Phew, I can breathe again.

Whiston Hospital is a huge acute care hospital in St. Helen's. I am put in the pediatric ward. The ward is big and has approximately twenty beds in it. In the middle of the room is a large rectangular table. Each family brings in fruit as it is healthy for their child to have.

Everyone puts the fruit in a pile in the middle of the table, and each child can eat whatever they want. This ward is a co-ed ward. Since food is in such shortage, we share what we have. On this table, there are also bottles of Lucozade. It comes in a long, tall bottle and it is an energy drink sold in the UK. It is for anyone to drink. Family members bring them in. It is good for rehydration and energy. Even at home when I am sick mum always gives me a drink of Lucozade. If we get too rowdy, the matron (nurse) comes in and yells at us to quiet down.

There isn't anything to do in the ward, so we make our own fun. There is a boy in the bed beside mine, and we like to joke around with each other. His name is Ian Coffee. He is in for something to do with his appendix. I tease him and call him Ian Tea.

He calls me Dosey Rosey. We banter back and forth like this. We become friends in the hospital, and keep each other company. He gets his pillow and hits me with it, I also hit him with mine, and before long we will all be in a pillow fight with everyone in our ward.

We hear the heavy sound of feet stomping coming our way. The laughter and giggles from all of us can be heard echoing all over the ward. There is only one person that can stomp her feet that loud, "Uh oh we're in trouble. It's the Matron." Of course, the ward matron comes in and she tells us to be quiet. She is no fun.

The matron wears a blue dress, white apron and a fancy hat that sits on her head. There are stripes around the bottom of her sleeves to distinguish that she is the matron. A doctor will not enter a ward room without first getting permission from the Matrons to enter. The nurses wear blue dresses with a white apron and black stockings and shoes.

I end up staying in the hospital for nine days until the meningitis is gone. I am very lucky to survive from this. I start to get better and gain the weight back. I am so grateful that I can return to being a normal, healthy child again. Everyone is glad to have me home. Mum and my siblings pitch in to help out with my recovery at home. I am still too sick to be going outside to play as I usually do, so I recover in the house.

When I get better, it is too late for my mum to register me for the beginning of Grade Three in school. Everyone has left for the summer holidays. My mum and I did not realize that I needed to do that. Neither one of us would think that it would be a big deal, but it turns out that it is. It is time to return to school in a fortnight (two weeks).

Chapter 6
The Wooden Compass and Belt

Today is the first day of school again. I wake up, get dressed and head out the door. I still have this sick feeling in the pit of my stomach of fear, dread; that things will still be the same. My heart is pounding out of my chest. My breathing is rapid with every step I take walking down the road. I have this overwhelming fear the abuse will continue. In my head, are my thoughts hoping I will be fine this year and happy. I repeat over and over, "Rose just do your work, learn a lot and be healthy." I keep playing it over and over like a tape recording. One can hope, right? So, I hope. It is not meant to be. I open the front doors of the school and walk to my classroom door.

I enter the classroom and immediately walk over to where the teacher is standing. He is standing near his desk, back to me. Immediately he turns around towards me. I can see that he is a tall, stocky man, bald patch on the top of his head, with grey hair and he is approximately fifty-nine years old. I notice he is wearing a suit, with a collar and tie. He tells me his name is Mr. Howard.

He begins to ask me who I am, and what I am doing in his classroom. I tell him, “My name is Rose Arnold, and I am in your Grade Three class.” He checks his list of students and does not see my name on his list. He makes it very clear that he has not been informed. He points me to an empty desk and I go and sit down.

He then calls me to the front of the classroom. He asks me to hold out my hands to him. At this moment I have no understanding why he wants me to do that. I hold out my hands in front of me. He tells me to hold them with my knuckles facing up. A huge wave of anxiety comes over me. He turns around and proceeds to pick up a wooden compass that is lying near the chalkboard. I see him pick it up and start walking towards me. I tense up not knowing what he is going to do with it at that time. I have done nothing to anger him.

I think to myself that he is going to hit me with it, and hit me he did. I tense up and hold myself as still as I can. I am terrified, not knowing what I have done wrong that he is doing this to me. I can see he is angry, his lips are pursed, and his face is getting red. He is angry that no one has informed him that I am joining his class. It is not my fault that my name wasn't on his class list, but he doesn't care.

He raises his arm with the compass in his hand and he brings it down. I can hear the crack as it hits my knuckles. The compass consists of two large wooden arms joined at the middle with a washer and a nut. It is solid wood and heavy. It is used for drawing circles on a blackboard.

It has a pointed tip on one side, and the other side you put in a piece of chalk. We have blackboards, and this is where he draws circles for our math classes.

I can only describe my beating as the most painful thing I have ever encountered. Is there a good enough reason why he is doing this? He thinks I am not following his rules? What are his rules? I can't believe he is doing this to me. This is only my first day of school.

My hands and knuckles are bleeding from the blows, the pain is unbearable. Welts are starting to form. I stand there and take it. If I say anything about it I will get hit more. I have to take the punishment. I proceed to go back to my desk and sit down.

This is the wooden compass used to discipline me, closed, and struck on the knuckles.

The second form of punishment that Mr. Howard has at his disposal is his leather belt. He uses that often to discipline the students in the class. That is his favorite form of punishment, especially to the boys in my class. Caning is always done across the knuckles or if the belt is used across the back of the legs. Tom Kelly is another boy who is also abused and punished by Mr. Howard.

Tom Kelly and John Thorogood are the two boys he picks on the most. John and I are friends and we hang out at recess and after school. I don't know much about Tom other than by the way he looks. Times are tough for him too. It is recess time so we head outdoors. My hands are still throbbing from the beating I took. John can see I'm upset. My knuckles are so sore. He comes over, gives me a nudge, and wants me to chase him around the playground.

Do they take me to the nurse's office over my knuckles and hands? No, they sure don't. I head back into class to finish the rest of the day. When I get home, I do not tell mum. I keep my hands away from her sight as best I can. She does not notice. I have dodged a bullet.

John always shows up at school with dirty hands because he swings on the gas lamp poles on his way to school. Mr. Howard sees his dirty hands and makes him come up to the front of the class. After humiliating him in front of all of us, he takes his belt out of his pants and straps John with it across the back of his knees. John winces in pain with his eyes scrunched shut as he endures every smack of the belt. Thank goodness Mr. Howard can't see his facial expressions. John does not dare to complain about it or show any type of emotion or Mr. Howard will strap him more.

At recess, it is my time to console John and I do. We are both the victims of his abuse. What a terrible thing we both have in common but, we do.

John's only error is being spontaneous, having fun and swinging on those gas lamp poles on the way to school. He pretends he is King Kong swinging from them.

We should be able to be kids, without a care in the world. We love running outside around the playground and love playing tag. He enjoys climbing the playground equipment; I play skipping with the girls. Soon it will be time to go back to class. We are not looking forward to that.

When John and I play together we are two friends having fun. Forgetting all the troubles we face. We are two friends or mates, as we call each other, not two victims. Victims we are though, through no fault of our own. Tom Kelly is also in our class. I do not hang around with Tom outside of class so I don't know a lot about him.

Tom gets the belt for not paying attention, if he spells words wrong or any reason the teacher can find. He and John always wear a shirt or t-shirt to class with short pants. This is how boys dress for school. They never wear long pants until they get to high school.

Boys' pants reach above the knee cap. This is the perfect spot for the teachers, especially Mr. Howard, to strap them. The boys wince in pain from the attack.

They are not allowed to show any emotions, but I know they want to cry. The pain from it is unbearable. I also wanted to cry. We take the beatings and say nothing.

I get caned or strapped for spelling mistakes, coming to class late, or not paying attention. If they ask you a question you cannot answer, you get caned. Abuse is a common daily occurrence at school. Any student that the teachers feel do something wrong, out comes the belt or the wooden compass, and we get hit with it. We try to make sure we don't do anything wrong.

The teachers are never reported for any of this. We're too scared and embarrassed to tell our parents, and the headmistresses never tell the parents. I can only imagine how many other children in England endure the same punishments we do.

The only relief we get from Mr. Howard's abuse is recess, lunch hours and then when the bell rings and it is time to go home. We are on pins and needles all day long. How can anyone learn in an environment like that? It's hard, believe me.

I walk my little sister Jean to school. She is so slow and I get annoyed with her. Thank goodness I make it back to school on time or I know I'll be in trouble again. Jean is two years younger than me, has long wavy brown hair. I have to pull her and keep saying, "Hurry up." as we head down the street.

I have an older sister named Vera. Vera is a different story. With Vera, I am always late for class and get strapped many, many times. Vera has epilepsy. She suffers with it all her life. I walk with her to the canteen and back for lunch. On the way back to school, there are two girls in Vera's class who always bully her. This is our quality time. We hold hands and head to the cafeteria. We arrive okay but never leave the same way.

The two girls in Vera's class are not very nice. Their names are Dorothy Paige and Gwen Hamlet. They are tall, always well dressed and mean. They always have their hair nicely brushed with ribbons in their hair. They always have polished shoes. They are bullies in school and outside of school.

The two girls always startle Vera and she ends up having an epileptic seizure. They seem to find this funny. I sure don't. They stand, jump towards her yelling Boo, and begin to start laughing at her, calling her horrible names. She is my sister; I am her protector. I get into so many fights protecting her from the bullies; knowing that I will get caned because it makes me late.

They are much taller than I, but I do not care. No one picks on my big sister, especially these two bullies.

When Dorothy or Gwen isn't looking, I bring my arm up as fast and hard as I can and punch them in the face. Sure, I take some bruises, but I am shorter, faster, and full of rage. I give them what they dish out. I do not like these girls at all.

Heading back to school, there are nettle bushes. They line the front yards of many homes, beside the sidewalk. They have very sharp nettles that sting your skin. Dorothy and Gwen often push Vera and me into them. The pain from those bushes is terrible. They dig into your skin and burn like heck. They are very painful. Vera and I always have rashes all over our arms, legs, and torsos from these bushes. This happens daily it seems.

Of course, I end up getting back to class late and once again, Mr. Howard canes me with the compass because I am late. Even though he can see the rashes all over me, he doesn't care. I am late, and in his mind, I deserve a cane, so the cane I get. He doesn't ask what happened to me since he doesn't care.

I have not told you anything so far about my brother William. Everyone calls him Billy. He is slow after suffering a depletion of oxygen to his brain when he is born.

He is the only boy in the household. Billy is at a different school along with Vera. The girls at school and boys never pick on Billy, only Vera. They are in special classes for children with disabilities.

I get through Grade Three and the summer holidays are upon us. Summer holidays I work; not having fun as other children do. Even though I am only nine years old I know I have to do whatever I can do to help provide more money for my mum. I am like superman, big and tough and strong, I have it set in my mind that I can do anything. And I do.

Chapter 7
Nine Years Old and My First Job

This year I decide to get my first job. I am going to be picking coal. Three doors down from my house is an elderly lady named Mrs. Hatton. She is in her sixties, about 5 feet tall with salt and pepper hair. She is stout, has a husband called Joe and a daughter Dorothy. Mrs. Hatton is a friend of my mum, so we end up befriending each other and go out picking coal, wood, peas, and potatoes. I know it is going to be a sweaty, dirty job but mum needs coal for the winter. None of us want to be cold, so I decide to go do it.

I am out the door at 6 am and I knock on Mrs. Hatton's door. She greets me all dressed in her dress, shoes and always wearing a black coat. She brings along a pram (baby carriage). She uses it for putting the coal in to bring home.

I know it is going to be a long, tiring day but I have to do it for my mum so we can have enough coal for the fire. We have to walk about three miles to reach the coal pit, but we walk it.

Off we go to with Mrs. Hatton is pushing the pram, inside it are many burlap bags to put the coal in, along with a pick and hammer. We are both singing as we walk to the pit. We truly enjoy spending time together. She tells me stories of when she was a little girl. I love hearing her stories and all she has to share. She is a very sweet lady, and I learn a lot from her.

We are enjoying each other's company along the way. She asks me about school, and she tells me about her family. Soon enough, here we are at the coal pit. It is big. It is approximately the width of two houses, and it is also about 50 to 60 feet deep. We reach the pit and I look down into the big hole. Mrs. Hatton is old and cannot climb up and down it or retrieve the coal, so I will do the work.

To retrieve the coal, I need to use a hammer or a pick. I venture to the side of the hole and climb down into the pit and fill up a bag of coal. I am scared to go down; the coal is slippery but I slowly lower myself to the bottom and I start chipping away. Getting back up is the hard part. I use all the strength I can muster in my legs to push me up as I cling to whatever rock I can until I make it to the top. I bring each bag back up the hole and put it in the pram. I make eight trips up and down. Mrs. Hatton stays at the top with the pram so no one will steal the coal we have. I do this over and over until we have eight-bushel bags full.

When I come up the final time, I look at Mrs. Hatton and she starts laughing. I am a sight for sore eyes. I am so dirty from the black soot, sweaty and tired; she tells me I look like no one owns me. She and I walk home. I am stiff and sore and cannot wait to get through the front door and have a bath. We make this trip about two times this summer. We get back to her house and I put four bags of coal in her shed outside. I take the other four bags home to my house for my family.

We realize we also need wood and we know of a great place to get a bit of wood for both of us. There is a big employer in St. Helen's called Pilkington's. They are a glass company and make a lot of products.

They make anything from glass such as ashtrays, drinking glasses, vases, even windscreens for automobiles. Behind the company is a huge pile of leftover wood they called a wood tip. This wood tip is approximately two miles from our homes.

Again at 6 am I am knocking on Mrs. Hatton's door. With pram in tow, off to the wood tip pile we go. Once we arrive, I go and grab the burlap bags out of the pram, climb up the woodpile and fill them with pieces of wood. The wood is heavy, I get slivers and my arms and hands are sore from the weight of them. It is a tiring workday but I collect eight bags of wood. Once collected, I load them in the pram again and off we go walking home. Once more, I give four bags to Mrs. Hatton and take the remaining four bags home to my mum. I put them in the coal shed with the coal that we had already collected the first time we went.

Everyone has enough to keep them warm all winter. We never get snow but we have a lot of rainy days and nights and it is cold and damp. Several farms are not far from us. This is another way to earn some extra money for Mrs. Hatton and my mum. Peas are the first harvest of the season, so Mrs. Hatton and I decide to go pea picking. The farm we go to is about a mile and a half from home. Closer than the other two places we went to. We venture out at 8 am to go picking. The farmer greets us when we get there and shows us which row he wants each of us to pick. We can both do the work this time. We each grab a hamper from the farmer, and we proceed to walk to the row we are picking. It is easier work, not as hard as picking coal and wood.

My best friend lives next door to Mrs. Hatton and her name is named Kathleen Smith. I ask Mrs. Hatton if Kathleen can come pea picking with us as she also wants to do it.

Mrs. Hatton tells me that Kathleen is lazy, not a hard worker like I am, so she tells me no, so Kathleen never comes with us.

We pick the row until our hamper is full. We leave it when full, and proceed down the row. Mrs. Hatton and I love peas. We eat more than we pick, so our pay is not what it should be. We do have a break for lunch at noon. Mum has sent me with a bread, butter, and jelly butty for lunch. The farmer makes a kettle of tea, so Mrs. Hatton and I sit down and eat our lunch and have a drink of tea. It's then time to go back to picking. It is hard on the back and the knees but we work hard.

We make about 2 pounds a day. That is about $4.00 Canadian. By the time we walk home, our bellies are aching from eating all the raw peas, but we don't care. They are delicious.

I have money to give my mum to buy extra potatoes, bread, and eggs for the family. That is all that matters to me. I do this until the season for pea picking is over.

I could have stopped there but I didn't. I still want to make money for the family so as always, Mrs. Hatton and I decide to go potato picking. Now, this job is harder than the peas. The farmer uses his plow to turn over the potatoes for picking.

The same thing happens as with the pea picking. We fill a hamper with the potatoes. When full, we leave the bag, grab another empty one and start filling again. This job is dirty because of the soil. My hands are very dirty when I get home. My back is aching from bending over all day. I ate a jam butty for lunch and the usual cup of tea from the farmer. I make about the same amount of money that I received from pea picking.

All the jobs are back-breaking, dirty, tiring jobs but it is worth it. We can afford to treat everyone to some little extras, some extra candy, extra margarine, or bread. Mum is always thankful for what I do to help out. I do it every summer as a child. As soon as I get home I hand her all the money I have made.

I play outside during the summer when I'm not working. I enjoy skipping or hanging out with my siblings and John Thoroughgood. School is fast approaching again and I will be entering senior level now. I am almost turning eleven.

The big event this summer is the future Queen's upcoming coronation on the Second of June.

I do not want to return to school because I know I will get caned or humiliated again for any reason the teachers see fit. My home is my sanctuary. I have a loving, caring mum and siblings to protect me and look after me. This is my safe haven. I cherish my home life.

This school year is the same as the others. I get caned for nothing as usual, but I get through it. This is my main goal this year. I am almost ready to start high school.

Well, school is finally over for the year. You don't know how happy I am. I cannot wait to get out of here and do fun things. It is going to be a fun day today. Finally, I have one thing to look forward to. It is our year-end Games Day. I cannot get to school fast enough today. I am skipping on the sidewalk and singing the whole way to school. Today it does not matter if I am well off or poor; I can let my hair down, and be free and have fun.

It is a day of fun. I can be a kid, finally. I am ecstatic. It lasts the whole day until the final bell. The games are fun. There are sack races, egg and spoon races, relay races, normal distance races and skipping races. I can't wait to do the skipping rope races. I am teamed up with someone else. The assistants tie a rope around each of our ankles. We have to run like this to the finish line. I didn't finish first but I run with all the energy I can muster up.

I win one race that day, the running race. I am so proud I finally accomplished something good. I am lined up in my track with the other runners. The gun goes off, and run I did. My feet almost can't keep up with the rest of me but I run.

I line up to receive my first place ribbon. Boy, it looks so good on my dress. I can't wait to show it to my mum. I have to admit that I got my mind in win mode by remembering all the horrible things my teachers did to me. That gives me the drive.

I can't wait to get home. I run in the door and kiss my mum and am elated that I won and am finally at home with my family. I can put all my troubles behind me. School is over.

Today is the day of the Coronation. The local legion has donated tables so we line them up and down the street. I'm talking about six blocks in length, tables end to end. It is very long. White paper tablecloths are covering them. The money (two crown) the lady had collected earlier in the year went to buying food. The tables are full of cakes, pastries, butties, sausage rolls, pork pies, jello, you name it. I help with setting up the tables. None of us have a TV so we sit at our tables and listen to the coronation. We sit down in our chairs, eat, and have a wonderful time.

I have never seen our street look so pretty. Union Jack flags, bunting; special signs for the Queen hang from poles, fences, and gates.

The street looks amazing all covered in red, white, and blue. Everyone is having a great time. We have tons of food and tons of fun.

Everyone is talking to each other, laughing, having a good time. The kids are playing with each other. Everyone is proud to be British that day. The coronation is amazing. We have a Queen now instead of a King.

After the coronation is over, whatever food is left, we can take home. Each person in England is given a metal tin with the Queen's picture on it and the date of the coronation. It is full of candy. I cannot remember picking it up.

Everyone in the street cleans up, grabs whatever they want and we all go back to our homes. It has been a wonderful day. Our bellies are full; it's time to go home.

Again, another summer is upon us. I work again in the coal pit, wood tip, and farms with Mrs. Hatton. This is how I spend most of my summer.

It keeps me busy and out of trouble too. At least I know in my heart my mum has extra money for other things for us. I love mum and will do any menial job to help her out. I work to give her everything I earn. She, in turn, gives me about 2 cents so I can go to the picture show on a weekend. I enjoy going to town to watch the black and white movies. Usually a couple of friends and I go there.

Chapter 8
Rose Begins High School

The year is 1954 and I am getting ready to start high school. I am 11 years old now. My high school is called Rivinton Road High School. It is mandatory when you are in high school that you have to wear a uniform. Somehow my mum finds enough money to buy me a uniform. This school is farther away than what St. Matthews was, so I have to take a bus to school.

My uniform consists of a brown skirt and a yellow shirt. I also wear a brown and yellow striped tie and a brown blazer. Brown socks also. They do not care about what colour shoes we wear. On the left breast pocket, there is the crest of the school sewn on it.

I wake up early and I cannot wait to put on my new uniform. I have never worn a uniform before. This is such a new experience for me. I am wearing a tie? Men always wear ties, but here I am putting on my first tie. I have to admire myself in the mirror. It feels so strange to me. I am ready and out the door I go. At this moment, my life is going to be one hundred percent different now that I am starting high school.

I arrive at school and find my classroom. I go into the class. I find a seat and sit down. The teacher is reading the rules, and schedules.

On the first day of school, each class they divide into four groups. The four groups are the Windsor group, whose colour is red. Buckingham is blue, Sandringham is yellow, and Balmoral is green. I am put in the Balmoral group.

Of course, like any other student, I want to be in the Windsor or Buckingham group. Whatever house you get put into; you are in that house all during school. If there are competitions of any kind, this is your competing team.

Our classes consist of reading, writing, arithmetic, PE or gym, history, geography, swimming, and music. To print or write, we use inkwells and quill tipped pens. Our classroom has a big blackboard where the teacher writes the lessons on it with chalk. My favourite subject is history.

I enter the music class. I want so much to play the tambourine. Our teacher is Miss Hall. Miss Hall starts handing out the instruments to the class. I end up with the triangle. I ask her if I can play the tambourine. This is all I have ever wanted to play. She tells me no. I am crushed.

To the girls she likes, she gives the tambourines. They don't even want to play them. They start complaining they want to play the piano or a stringed instrument.

I want to play it. I am stuck with the triangle, so I play it with my heart and soul put into it. What choice do I have, at least I have an instrument to play? It could have been worse I suppose.

Next class I have is PE class, better known as gym class. I am looking forward to participating in the PE class. The gym teacher is a young woman, in her thirties. Her name is Miss Taylor. Galoshes are a rule (gym shoes). Whoever can't afford to have a pair of these galoshes cannot take part. Of course, that is me.

Miss Taylor lines up all the girls. I know someone in PE class too that is my friend, so things have to be better, or so I think and hope. Carol is a friend of mine and my younger sister, Brenda. We hang out together all the time. Carol is a ton of fun. Carol is tall, thin and one of two twins. She has shoulder-length brunette hair and blue eyes.

During PE class, Carol and I are not allowed to take part in it because we don't have galoshes (running shoes) to wear. Instead, I have to sit on the floor and am not allowed to take part. I keep my feelings bottled up, do not say anything but not Carol. She is feistier than I am. Carol punches this teacher in the mouth over it and she gets suspended for three days. After the years of abuse, I want to cheer or laugh but I don't dare. In my head I am saying, "What a good job Carol, she deserves it."

I am not able to play football (soccer), netball, track and field or anything. So much for our well being, promoting good health to their students; they did not care. I have never been so bored in my life. Wow, is this class over yet?

You come from a poor house and you know it. It still stings like a bee sting to my heart. I am completely helpless. I am alone in my fight. They do not look past the fact that I am still human. No one cares. They have no heart or compassion to let me take part in things. I hate school, hate it. I do not want to ever go back, but I have to attend until I am fifteen years old.

Cooking class or what is also known as home economics is another class I am looking forward to doing. My teacher whose name I cannot remember is a short, overweight German-speaking woman. I cannot wait to learn how to cook and bake. For the cooking class, we have to bring ingredients with us to use. I don't have the ingredients to bring in, so I am again not allowed to partake in the cooking classes. I plead with her to take part, but she will not allow me to. Instead of being able to cook, I am told to clean. We all wear aprons in class. I am like Cinderella in a room full of evil stepsisters, with my teacher being the evil step mum.

What do I get to do in class? I get to clean the stoves by myself. They have to be sparkling clean. There are four stoves, four fridges in the classroom. I have to clean everything, and the girls make a mess.

I must clean insides of the fridges, mop the floors, wipe the counters, and clean out the cupboards and pantry room. Whatever needs cleaning, I clean. It is so wrong, but there is nothing I can do about it. I put my gloves on, grab the cleaning supplies and off I go. My clothes are dirty from grease, dirt and are wet from the water.

The teachers are the authority, they make the rules, so I do not dare argue and complain about it. I know if I do, I will be caned. The class smells so good from all the food being cooked. The room is full of laughter.

It pains me to see all the girls of privilege cooking. Why can't I? I am capable of learning how to cook and bake. I want to learn so much, I am dying to get over to the station and make something so I can take it home and share with the family. I am heartbroken about it. I get stuck with all the sweaty, dirty jobs to do.

That is why I am engrossed watching my mum bake on Sundays. This is the only way I can ever learn how to make pastry for pies and cook or bake anything. I sure can't learn it at school. I make sure every time mum cooks and bakes I am right beside her watching and learning. As I am growing older, she lets me help out more. Soon I am rolling dough and making pastry. She even lets me make the pies for our dinners.

This teacher also gives my younger sister Jean a hard time. She also teaches sewing class. Jean one day loses her sewing needle and tells the teacher. The teacher makes her get on her knees and look in between every wooden floorboard until she finds the needle. Jean never does.

I am an average student; always get B level grades throughout school. I work hard but I hate everything about school.

I seem to get along with the teachers in geography, writing and history. Nothing significant stands out in my mind. There is one more class that does stand out though, and as you can guess, not in a good way.

Once a week we have swimming lessons. We go to our local baths called Boundary Road Baths for our swimming lessons. One rule to swim is to have a bathing cap. A female cannot go into the pool without one. I bet you can guess who doesn't have one and is not allowed to go swimming lessons either? That is right, me. Any other females in my class can't take lessons either if they don't have this cap.

Again I am left to sit on the side of the pool and watch everyone else learn how to swim. Why am I even here? I would rather be at home. I need to know how to swim and I want to be in there learning.

I have no knowledge of my siblings being abused like I am in school. Only one sister, my younger sister Jean experienced an issue in her sewing class I have written in the high school years. As I have said, no one talks about it. A child does not confide it to a parent or sibling.

Chapter 9
Holiday Festivities I Enjoy

There is one week preparation for a particular night we celebrate every year. November 5th in England is Guy Fawkes Night. He and other conspirators attempted to burn down the Houses of Parliament. It was thwarted after someone told the authorities about their plot.

The other conspirators were either killed resisting capture or, like Fawkes; they were tried, convicted, and executed. In the aftermath, Parliament declared November 5 a national day of thanksgiving, and the first celebration of it.

For a week before this, the children go house to house and ask for 1 pence (2 cents) for Guy Fawkes Night. With all the money gathered, they buy fireworks out of it. Some children take a shirt from their dad; another takes a pair of pants. They use a burlap bag and stuff it with papers, whatever they can find. They do not put a face on it. Instead, they carry this effigy while going door to door for donations. On the night of the 5th of November, everyone makes a huge pile out of wood and set him on fire.

When the fire is nice and big they throw the effigy of Guy on top of the pile and watch him burn and celebrate. They also set off fireworks. This is an annual tradition in the UK. Everyone participates in it.

It seems every holiday someone steals our front wooden gate to use for this occasion. Mum has to go to the local phone box and call the local council to ask them to come and bring another gate to replace it. Whoever is stealing them is doing it to others on the street too, but ours is always targeted.

All our things are ready for the night. Our effigy is made. We all start piling up wood in the field behind our house to use for the pyre. Darkness is here. We get our coats on as it's cool in November. Boots are also a must. We head outside and the boys begin to light our bonfire. The fire is ablaze. One of the boys then toss Guy Fawkes on the fire and we watch him burn up. We're all yelling and cheering and lighting the fireworks. Everyone is having a good time.

The field is full with everyone out celebrating. The fireworks banging and bursting in the sky is the highlight of the night. The fires are out and it's time for bed. I run up to my room. I am dog tired and climb into bed. It doesn't take long for me to fall asleep. It is hot beside the fire; I can hear the crackling of the wood and embers. It looks so beautiful burning, the orange and yellow glow from the flames.

Another holiday I always look forward to is Christmas. We are able to buy decorations and we always make paper streamers to hang from the tree. On Sundays, we sit around the kitchen table and make paper chains for the tree and walls. Foil made ornaments that look like baubles or bells hang from the ceiling.

We have a small artificial tree that we put on top of the mantle. We decorate it with ornaments, tinsel, and lights. It looks so pretty in the house.

We never get toys for Christmas. Not with seven children in the house. We have a stocking that we hang from the mantle for the morning.

I wake up Christmas morning excited to see what Father Christmas has left for me. I look inside and find a couple of candies, an apple and a bar of chocolate in it. It also contains a reading book and colouring book and crayons.

We are all so happy with what Father Christmas has brought us. We spend the day playing outside or in the kitchen trying to help mum make the Christmas dinner.

Before dinner, we all sit in the living room around the radio and listen to the Kings Christmas radio speech. It is the Queen who will broadcast after she becomes Queen in 1953. It's dinner time. Mum and my older sisters have made a rabbit with all the fixings. We have to sit at two tables to eat because there are so many of us. Mum sits with the older siblings. I sit at the kiddies table.

Mum puts our plate on the table in front of us. I can smell delicious roasted rabbit, mashed potatoes, cabbage, Yorkshire puddings, and gravy. It smells so good. I eat it all. For dessert, we eat a trifle, mincemeat tarts, bread pudding and sausage rolls. I take my dinner plate to the kitchen and we all pitch in to do the dishes.

At the end of the meal, it is always a tradition that we pull crackers. Inside the cracker, there is a small novelty and a tissue paper hat that we put on our head. We all look silly, but we don't care. You can't finish an English Christmas dinner without doing this tradition.

We laugh and giggle over the silly jokes that come inside the crackers. We also like to trade the novelties we find inside. I get an eraser from my older sister Ellen, and I give her a pair of nail clippers in return.

We've all had a busy day, so we get ready for bed and turn in for the night. The rest of the week is either playing outside or catching up with homework. The next big day to come is New Year's Eve. We all spend the night at home waiting for the clock to strike twelve. We gather a slice of bread, a piece of coal and a coin. This represents food, heat, and money for the year. At 11:59 pm we give the items to the darkest haired male that is in the home. He, in turn, goes out the back door with the items.

At exactly midnight he knocks on the front door and whoever opens it has to let him in. This will bring good luck to all for the coming year.

It is the one-night mum lets us all stay up late. We all hold hands in a circle and sing Auld Lang Syne at midnight, then give each other a hug and a kiss, and then it's time for bed.

After the Christmas holiday break, it is time to go back to school. All I want is to get through every day as best I can and finish. I make it through school and am now fifteen.

Easter is here and we are so excited we can get something for our mum. Easter Sunday we all trek down to the church for the service. They hand out a daffodil to everyone who is there. With eight of us we have quite a nice bouquet for mum to take home with her and put it in the house.

It is now June, I am done. I am so happy I cannot contain myself. I cannot run home fast enough. It is a Friday and for the first time in a long time, I have nothing to do this weekend except be glad I am free.

Chapter 10
School Finished
Now Off To the Workforce

I finish school on Friday, and start working on a Monday, which is July 1st. I get hired as a factory worker for a company called Tinlins. They are a book binding company. I begin as a line worker. My job is to get the books after they are bound and pack them in boxes for shipping.

I work there for about eighteen months. When it is payday I bring home my pay and give it all to mum. That is what you do. Mum gives me a bit of money back. I can take the bus to work every day, and have a few shillings left over to go to the movies. My sisters do the same thing. By this time, the older sisters are married and in their own homes. Jean and I are working. On payday, we get a sealed envelope with money in it. I earn 1 pound 2 shillings. It equals about $1.80 per week.

I love my sister Jean, but she is demanding. I start work before Jean does, so I am the first one to get home. Mum is busy making tea (supper) when I get home. By this time, I am hungry of course. I ask mum when tea will be ready.

She tells me that tea is almost done but she has to feed Jean first. I complain to mum that I am home first, I should have it first. She tells me, "Well you know Jean. If I don't have her tea done when she walks in the house, she will have a fit." I always have to wait to eat because of her. It is so unfair.

This angers me, of course, but I do not want Jean getting upset with mum so, I wait. This goes on for years. I wait to eat. It saves many arguments from occurring. If Jean is happy, we are all happy. Oh well, I have to wait another fifteen minutes for my food. I am eating, that is the main thing.

Chapter 11
Starting to Date

I am sixteen years old, not looking for romance or anything more. My life is busy with work and bringing home my pay to my mum. At work, I am always told how beautiful I am, but I do not let it go to my head. I focus on work. I have shoulder length wavy brown hair and blue eyes along with a slim build.

While I am working there, I meet a co-worker called Tony Finnegan. He seems very interested in me. We go out on a few dates but there is no spark on my end. I am sixteen now. He seems to be too forward for my liking. After a few dates, he asks me to marry him. I dump him that day. I do not want to get married at sixteen years of age.

There is another guy that works at Tinlin's. He is going through his apprenticeship to be a millwright. He is about 5 feet 8 inches tall, with dark brown hair, and dark brown eyes and thin. His name is Glynn Jones. He goes around fixing machines in the plant. I have caught his eye and don't know it. Glynn comes to work every day dressed in a suit and tie. He then puts a set of coveralls over his suit when he starts to work.

There is a machine that looks like a sewing machine. The machine operator sews the pages of the books together. It is then sent to a different department to have the pages trimmed to book size. I get the pages and pile them on a pallet before they go to the trimming department.

During work hours I often see the electricians or mechanics doing their job in the factory. One of them stops where I work and hands me a note every day. It is a note from Glynn asking me to go out on a date with him. I tell the workers to tell him to get lost. I am not interested.

After I leave Tinlin's, I start working in the cafeteria at a company called the BICC. It is a huge company. The name stands for British International Callenders Cables. Thousands of employees work here. They manufacture paper insulated power cables under license from US patentees. They make paper-wrapped cabling for electricity.

The canteen is huge. There are different sections, and each section according to the departments where the workers are. They serve hot lunches, soups, butties, desserts, and beverages. The most popular beverage, of course, is tea.

My duties include various things. I wait for the employees to finish their meal, remove their dishes, and clean the tables. I never have to do the dish washing, someone else does that job. I enjoy working here. It is a great place to work.

To get back and forth from work I take the bus. Buses are finally a means of transportation. I start to notice that Glynn is always at the bus station at the same time I am. He takes a different one to his apprenticeship job at Tinlin's. This goes on for months.

One day, I see Glynn get on my bus. I am not sure what is going on. As I am ready to get off the bus he comes my way and won't let me get off it until I agree to go on a date with him. I finally agree.

I remember this particular day at work, winning employee of the month. My picture is hanging on the wall for everyone to see. I have blue eyes, shoulder-length brunette hair curled into a coif. People often stop me at work and say that I should enter a beauty contest, and that I am that beautiful. I am too shy to do anything like that.

At the BI as we called it for short, I have a good friend called June Qualters who also works in the canteen with me. We like to hang out, outside of work hours also. She is the same age as me; we have a lot in common. On the weekends, June likes to check out the local clubs in Liverpool. I am into music coming out of America. I listen to Elvis Presley and other singers. June likes to go out. She keeps inviting me to this particular club located on Matthew Street in Liverpool.

I ask June to tell me who the band is that she wants me to go and see with her. Where were they from? June says they are local Liverpool lads who are good. They are filling the club up every time they play. As I am more interested in American singers I keep refusing to go and never end up going. I remember saying to her, "Oh they'll never be popular," and I regret saying that. It turns out this band is from Liverpool.

They are playing at a club still famous called the Cavern Club. In the future, they take the world by storm. The band turns out to be none other than the Beatles. I have my chance to see them and I blow it.

Chapter 12
I Meet the Love of My Life

Glynn and I plan to meet up in Prescott for our first date. We have made plans to go to the picture show in Liverpool and see South Pacific. Of course that night it is foggy. You can't see two feet in front of you. In a Sherlock Holmes story when they mention fog as thick as pea soup, they are not exaggerating. It is very thick. I get on the bus from St. Helen's and take it to Liverpool. I wait there about an hour and he never shows up. Yes, as you can guess, I am upset.

Did I do something wrong? Is he playing games with me? Has he lost interest in me? I am very disappointed and a little angry but what can I do. I just have to wait to see if he speaks to me again.

Glynn and I manage to chat, and I find out that he couldn't meet me in Liverpool if he wanted to. He lives in a suburb of Liverpool called Huyton Roby. You have to hop on the bus to get into Liverpool since it is too far to walk. All the buses had stopped going to and coming out of Liverpool. He couldn't get one.

We make another date night. I get dressed up in my fancy white blouse, black and white pinstriped pencil skirt, and makeup. I can't afford nylons so I do what every young lady does, I get brown gravy powder and mix it with water and paint that on my legs. We all do it. I put on my coat, and off I go to the bus stop. There is Glynn looking dapper in a suit and tie.

We proceed to walk to the local picture theater and watch South Pacific. Finally, we get to see it. It is the big picture this year to watch.

We go out on dates on a Saturday. This is the only day Glynn has available. Because he is going in for his apprenticeship he has to go to night school two nights per week. Other nights are homework or whatever other plans he has.

Usually, Glynn comes to my house and then we take the bus to Liverpool. We like to spend the afternoon shopping, then go somewhere for supper. Some nights we go to the picture show, or go for a walk. He then brings me back home and gets the bus back himself. He is a proper gentleman.

We court for about eighteen months before he asks me to marry him. He gets down on one knee and asks me. I tell him before I say yes, he has to ask my mum. So off we go to my mum's house and he asks her if he can marry me. Of course, my mum says yes.

Chapter 13
The Wedding Is Set

We set the wedding for September 25, 1962. It is a simple ceremony, only four of us in attendance. Before the wedding, we find a brand new house in Ashton-in-Makerfield that we want to buy. We contemplate whether to have a big wedding or use the money to put a deposit on the house.

We both decide to forgo the big wedding and instead put down a deposit on the brand-new house. It doesn't go over well with Glynn's dad. He wants us to have a big, huge, fancy wedding.

Before the wedding, Glynn's dad is very upset that he is marrying me. He tells Glynn that I am not good enough for him, so if he marries me, he will not go to the wedding. A little bit of history about Ernie, Glynn's dad. He served in Her Majesty's Navy while Glynn and his other siblings were small. Glynn's mother Edith dies when Glynn is 15. Edith is Ernie's second wife. His first wife Ruth had also died leaving four children without a parent at that time. Ernie sent the children to Wales for his mother Granny Jones to raise them. She had to raise them within her senior years.

The kids go to the Harpton Estate in Old Radnor Wales. The estate belongs to royalty. It is the stately home of Lord and Lady Duff-Gordon. Sir Cosmo is well known, for a bad reason it turns out.

He is the man that dressed up as a woman, got in lifeboat number one on the Titanic. He would come back to Wales and they lose everything. Glynn's dad thinks he is better than my family, but he does think I am trash because I am raised in a poor home. Glynn is furious. He loves me for me, not how I grew up. He loves my family also.

I am devastated at first, he does not like me because of growing up poor. Even he discriminates against me. Glynn is livid that he would treat me this way and say what he did say to me. It causes a big rift between the two of them. Since he won't attend our wedding, my mum decides not to as well. She feels weird going if he is not, so we tell her that it's okay, not to feel bad about it.

The only ones that are at the church are Glynn and me, my older sister Ellen, and her husband Gerald. I am dressed in a white skirt, with a white wool jacket to match. I wear a white pillbox style hat on my head, white high heel shoes, and carry a handbag instead of a flower bouquet.

Glynn is wearing a dark blue suit, with matching pants, black polished shoes, and a white shirt with a dark blue tie. He looks so handsome. I cannot take my eyes off of him. We say our vows and we are now husband and wife.

I keep up with the wedding tradition of something old, something new, something borrowed and something blue. I borrow the hat, wear a blue slip under my outfit, the old is my handbag, and new is my wedding outfit.

After we get married, we go to my mum's house and the five of us go out for a wedding breakfast. We eat at the Fleece Hotel in St. Helen's.

Our wedding breakfast is bacon, eggs, sausage, home fries, toast, beans, and sausage. It is a full English breakfast. We are all stuffed after finishing all that.

We all leave the restaurant and head back to our house so I can get my suitcase. It is time to start our honeymoon. I grab my suitcase, kiss my mum goodbye, and kiss my siblings. Glynn and I catch the bus at the end of the road at the roundabout; and take it to Blackpool for our honeymoon. It is hard to leave. My mum is crying her eyes out. I need to get out of here. There is a huge lump in my throat.

It is this moment it hits her that I am leaving home and will not be coming back there every night and living there. I am crying as I am running to catch the bus too.

Blackpool is a seaside resort on the Irish Sea coast of England. It's popular for family days out and honeymooning. Blackpool illuminations are an annual light show along the Promenade. There is a nine mile pier to walk. Along this walkway you can find bingo shops, restaurants, pubs, souvenirs. There is so much to do there one can never get bored. You can go swimming in the Irish Sea, lie on the beach, and even ride the donkeys that are on the beach.

Across the road from the beach is a road, and on the other side of the road are a slew of buildings. You can take a ride up to the top of Blackpool Tower, eat, and look out at the scenery. There are shows in the evening to go see, and you can also go bowling. There are also shops where they sell gag chocolates, and lots of fish and chip shops.

Our honeymoon is now over, time to take the bus to our new home. We arrive and Glynn is a total gentleman. He carries me over the threshold. Today is the beginning of our life together that will last fifty-five and a half years.

Ashton-in-Makerfield is a town in Greater Manchester area. It is approximately thirteen miles from Liverpool. Our home is a brick bungalow.

The town's main source of employment is coal mining. Glynn is still working at Tinlin's, and I am still at the BI. Every morning we take the train to Prescott; then I jump on one bus, Glynn on a different one into Liverpool. Each evening we would both meet up at the station and take the 5 o'clock train home.

Chapter 14
We Start Our Family

The year is 1963; I am expecting a baby in December. I am pretty sure it will be a boy so we have picked out the name David. Glynn has now finished up his apprenticeship and he starts working for a colliery (coal mine) here in town. It is less pay but closer to home for him. In my sixth month of pregnancy, I stop working at the BI and stay home until the baby is born.

I am preparing for the birth. Your first baby is born in a hospital, any other births after that are at home and you have with a midwife with you.

I am going into labor, so we head to the hospital. It is Billinge Maternity Hospital. It opened in 1948 and closed down to make way for a newer, more modern hospital in 2004. At 11:50 pm on December 8th I give birth to a daughter. Of course, we only have the name David picked out, thinking that she was going to be a male. We name her Gaynor. She is nineteen inches long, 7 lb 2 oz, and has a full head of dark brown hair.

The nurses on the maternity ward are calling her the Beatle baby, because of the amount of hair she has.

We take her home after five days. You have to stay at least five days to ensure mother and baby are healthy enough to go home. I decide after bringing the baby home that I am not going to go back to work anymore. I become a housewife.

Some days I take Gaynor on the train with me and head to St. Helen's to see my mum and sisters. I am particularly close to my younger sister Brenda. We can't go anywhere without Brenda being there. Believe me, that is a good thing. Brenda is the baby of the family.

She is short, chunky, has short dark brown hair, brown eyes, and has an infectious laugh. She usually wears a blouse or top with a mini skirt and sandals. She never wears pants. She can swear like a sailor, but has a heart of gold. She is very close to my mum. All of us are no longer living at home, except for Brenda and Billy. Brenda is their caretaker. She is such a great cook. She can make anything taste like it came out of a five star restaurant. My favourite dish of hers is a bacon, egg, and cheese pie. She often makes extras and gives me one to take home. She has a sweet tooth, is seen either eating a sweet or some creamy type of dessert.

You are always laughing when she is around. She is a go-getter, not afraid to do or try anything new. She is also close to my mum. Brenda takes care of my mum.

If I need to go shopping, Brenda is towing along with me to the shops. We do everything together. I go to visit her, and she comes to my house for a few days or overnight. You can see us all going for a walk. I have Gaynor in the pram. Every mother has a Silver Cross pram.

Two years later, I am pregnant with my second child. This time I have a midwife following my pregnancy. She comes and sees me at the house. All I have to do is ring her when I am going into labor. Well, Glynn has to go down the road to the telephone box to do that. The midwife gets called on November 13th, 1965. At 10:15 am, I give birth to our second daughter, we name Julie. She has blonde hair and blue eyes. She has very little hair when she is born, unlike Gaynor who had a full head of dark hair. She weighs 8 lb, 10oz.

My eldest, Gaynor, comes in to see her baby sister Julie minutes after she is born. Gaynor is sucking on a lollipop. She decides she will be a nice big sister and proceeds to put the lollipop in Julie's mouth to share with her. Julie is sucking away on it until the midwife sees what is going on, and gets mad at Gaynor and takes her out of the room. I am exhausted and it doesn't take long for me to fall asleep. Gaynor is jealous of having a baby sister and doesn't like me having to look after her baby sister. Sometimes, I find her shaking Julie's crib and I give her heck.

Life goes on. Glynn decides to get a job closer to home but with less pay. He starts working at a colliery (coal mine) as a millwright. Every night he comes home covered in soot from head to toe. All you can see is his lips, the white of his eyes and the palms of his hands. I know he doesn't want to work there but he does so he can be home with me and the girls much earlier in the evening.

I worry every day when he leaves, never knowing if the mine will explode or cave in or even if he will come home at night. I cannot let it bother me too much. I do not want it affecting him. Friday or

Saturday nights Brenda comes to visit and look after the girls.

There is a local club where the miners hang out, and we sometimes go there for a pint or a dance. They are always fun nights. The entertainment is always great. People get up and sing, play an instrument or do whatever they are good at. There are two singers that love to perform there. Their voices are amazing.

Little do I know now, but they go on to have a huge career in the music business. Their names are Engelbert Humperdink and Tom Jones.

Weekends we play with the girls, go to my mum's by train, go shopping, or take the girls in the pram to the park to play. Brenda and I like to go to town while Glynn takes in a local football game.

It is nineteen sixty-six and Gaynor is three now, Julie is one. Money is tight for us all. The pay from the mine is not a lot. I can see it is bugging Glynn. He is not happy.

Work at the mine is tough and dangerous. He tells me one day that he's fed up with the lousy pay and wants to try to give us all a better life in another country.

We go into Liverpool to check out our options. They mention two options to us that are trying to find licensed millwrights to come and work there. The two options are Cape Town, South Africa and Ontario, Canada. We ask a lot of questions about both countries. We come to decide that we want to try Cape Town. Glynn will have a job waiting for him. A house, car, housekeepers, and gardeners are part of the deal. That is a hard deal to pass on. We are leaning towards Cape Town until we find out some news that we don't like.

I like to do my own gardening and housekeeping. I don't like the thought of strangers in my home. I tell them that I don't want to hire outsiders and am immediately told I have to. It is impolite and disrespectful if I don't. I tell Glynn that I like to do my own cooking and cleaning. They end up telling us one bit of information that makes us turn down the idea of moving to Cape Town. They tell us that if Glynn is driving and happens to hit a black man, he is to run over him until he is dead. If not, he will have to pay the man's bills to the family for the rest of his life. No, that is not happening; Cape Town is off the table.

We take the girls and jump on the train to Liverpool again. From Lime Street Station we head over to Canada House to see what they have to offer. They inform us that there are a lot of Brits moving to Manitoba, and there are tons of jobs there. They are in desperate need of tradesmen.

They are bringing skilled people from all over Europe to work there. My sister Jean and her husband emigrate to Canada in April of 1967 and head to Winnipeg, Manitoba for work. We happen to talk to Jean and explain about us choosing to come to Winnipeg.

George informs us that there is no work there, Ontario has lots of jobs. Glynn and I then go back to Canada House and inform them there are no jobs in Manitoba. Ontario is where they are hiring. They say we can go to Ontario. They will pay our fares there but we have to pay the cost back monthly when we get there. We ask them what Canada is like. They tell us that summers are hot but do not mention anything about how cold the winters are.

We learn how big Canada is. They explain all the different provinces, lakes, etc. What I can do there for fun and what the schools are like for the girls. It all sounds good.

Glynn and I take the train back home, sit at the kitchen table, I make us tea, and we talk about our options. My family and I are super close, I don't want to leave England, but I love Glynn. He wants to go, so I support the decision he makes. He wants to move to Canada, so Canada is where we will soon live.

I head to St. Helen's to tell mum and the family of our decision. Mum is very upset. She begs me to leave the girls in England, she will look after them. She does not want to be that far away from Gaynor and Julie growing up. She states that Glynn and I go by ourselves and try it out and if we don't like it, come back to England. I am terrified of going. I have never flown on an airplane, so I don't know what to expect.

The date is set for November 6, 1967, for us to immigrate to Canada. We sell the house and pack our belongings in tea chests for the move. Before this date, our daughter Gaynor comes down with a very bad cold. I take her to the doctors and am told that the move will have to wait; they will not allow her travel. They worry that the cabin pressure might cause severe damage to her ears.

This summer we decide to take the kids on holiday to a resort called Butlins. I invite my sister Brenda to come along with us. All five of us get on the bus and head out to Skegness. We have rented a cabin room for all of us for four days of fun. We settle in and the girls go to see a play. There is so much to do here. There are activities for the kids, shows and movies for the adults. We head to one of many cafes and restaurants for our meals.

There is a full buffet breakfast and supper, as well as a restaurant that serves traditional English food and Indian dishes. The staff that works here are amazing. On nights when the adults are out having their fun, they have babysitters that come to your room and mind the children until you get back. There is also a full fairground for the kiddies, a beach, and live shows. You can swim in the pool. There is also a movie cinema and workshops for different ages. There are pubs where everyone that has a talent gets up and plays the piano, or another instrument or even sing. We meet up with a couple of women there who are also holidaying with their children and have a blast. We laugh until our faces are ready to fall off.

Gaynor is the talkative child of mine. Julie is quieter. For Christmas I buy Glynn a brand new watch. I think I am safe until Christmas; he won't find out about it. Then Gaynor decides to open her mouth. Glynn is coming home from work one night. Gaynor yells out the window as he walks by, "Guess what dad? Mum bought you a new watch for Christmas." I am so upset but can't show her how angry I am. So much for the element of surprise huh?

We head home after a great few days away and put our house up for sale. We cannot take the furniture with us, it's just too expensive, so we have to sell it and start again when we get to Canada. It doesn't take long for the house to sell. A lovely couple buys our house. They moved to Canada, ended up not liking it there and moved back to England. It is then, we move back into mum's house until it is time to leave.

Chapter 15
Moving to Canada

The time is fast approaching, it is December 5th. We are leaving in two days. Mum cannot stop crying. She cries until the time we leave. I am so sad for mum but we have to go now. Jean and George are waiting for us in Ontario. We leave on December 7th.

The morning of our departure we call a taxi to take us all to Manchester Airport for our new life. I kiss my crying mother goodbye. She gives the girls two golliwog dolls to take to Canada with them, and it's time to go. I tell mum, of course, I will bring us all back for visits to see her when we are able to.

My sisters Mary and Brenda come along in the taxi with us to the airport. We get checked in, and it's time to hug and kiss them goodbye. Our possessions are on the ship heading to Canada. We spend our last moments with Mary and Brenda, and go through Customs and wait for the flight. I cannot imagine life without them around every day but I am hoping and praying we will have a better life in Canada.

It is time for our flight. We all go through boarding and get on the plane. The flight leaves at 10 o'clock pm and arrives in Toronto, Ontario in the morning. Our flight is with BOAC. It stands for British Overseas Airways Corporation.

We are taxiing down the runway and I clutch the armrests until my knuckles turn white. I am scared to death. Soon we are up in the air. In the row behind us is another English couple headed to a city called Hamilton to live with their daughter.

Our Gaynor is quite the talker. For only being a day short of turning four she sure can talk. She keeps the couple behind us entertained by talking to them during the whole flight. The plane is to land in Toronto on the 8th of December. While we are flying across the Atlantic, they tell us there is a huge snowstorm in Toronto, so we cannot land there. They inform us that the plane will be landing in Montreal instead. We land in Montreal. This is now our port of entry, not Toronto.

BOAC is putting us up in a hotel for the night until we can catch another flight to Toronto in the morning. We find out that there was no snowstorm in Toronto, but the baggage handlers went on strike at midnight. The men have to unload the luggage from the plane themselves and carry it to the buses. We then get taken to the Holiday Inn for the night. I am tired, Glynn also, the kids are way past their bedtime.

We enter the hotel and get our room keys for the night. The airline has given us a coupon for a meal in the hotel. We take the suitcascs and thc girls up to the room and order soup and crackers for them.

They are hungry and cold. The girls go to bed and Glynn and I head down to the restaurant for our dinner. Everyone is angry that they lied to us.

We head down to the restaurant for a late-night meal. The adults order the most expensive meals on the menu. When it comes they are telling the staff that's not what they want, and they order something different. They are all angry that we were lied to, so they make sure the airline pays for the inconvenience.

Glynn and I are so tired we head to our room to sleep. We check on the girls and they are sound asleep. It's soon morning again and time to get ready for our flight to Toronto. We head down to the restaurant for breakfast before heading back to the airport. On our flight from Manchester we met a nice woman dressed in a big fur coat and big fur boots which I found out are mukluks.

She asked how our hotel room was and how we slept. I tell her that the room was so cold it was hard to fall asleep. She asks me if I turned the room's thermostat up high enough. After having lived in a house with only a coal fire for warmth, I ask her what a thermostat is. She explains that's how you get heat. No wonder we froze.

We get loaded onto the bus and off we go to Mirabel Airport. Today is a special day it's Gaynor's fourth birthday. Before leaving England my family threw Gaynor a birthday party. As we are taxiing down the runway, I see a huge yellow machine on the runway beside us with a big metal plow on the front of it.

I tap Glynn and say, "They must have a lot of snow in Canada, look at the size of that." Remember I said earlier they told us the summers are hot but nothing about how cold it is in winter; and how much snow there is there. None of us have any warm clothing for these temperatures. We all travel in our light jackets and shoes.

Here we are, at last, we land in Toronto. We go through customs, we are in Canada, do as Canadians do we are told. England is the mother country, not the other way around but I put that out of my mind. The doors finally open and there is my sister, Jean, and my brother-in-law, George, waiting for us.

They take our suitcases and we all get into the car for the drive to Brantford. I have no clue how far away Brantford is or anything about it.

We get to Jean's house and we all unwind. I don't know it yet but we are all going later to her sister-in-law's house for a birthday party for Gaynor. Talk about a lucky girl. She has two birthday parties this year. We're all tired, but we have a nice time, then it's time to head home. It doesn't take long to fall to sleep that night. Life begins in Canada. It is so cold here and is that snow? I have never seen snow in my life. The next day we all head to the shops to buy some winter coats and boots. We have no winter coats, boots, hats, or anything.

It is Monday morning and Glynn is to begin his new job at a company called Massey Ferguson. They make huge combines for farms. He works for approximately two weeks, and then they are informed that they are getting laid off. Glynn is frantic. He's in a new country with a wife and two children and no job. Why did we leave England to come to this? I don't like the snow, not at all. Glynn spends the next day job hunting. He gets hired on the spot at a company called Crane. They make bathroom fixtures. They make pipes, valves, and fittings as well as toilets. We can all breathe a sigh of relief again.

I get my first job not long after. I take the afternoon shift so I can be home with the girls during the day, and Glynn can look after them in the evenings. I start work at our local hospital as a cleaner. It is a hard, back-breaking job but I like it. I am instructed to clean the offices of the Pathologist, and the surgical theaters. I work there for extra money. My intentions are to use this money to pay for us all to go back to England for a vacation. I have saved up enough for our trip and ask my boss for time off. She refuses so I quit that day.

Glynn ends up getting offered a job to work for Pickering Nuclear Generating Station. Before he can start work, they want to send him up north to a small town called Deep River to go to school. We pack up, and off we go to Deep River for what is supposed to be a year. Glynn is at the school in Chalk River. We move into an apartment and I hate it. My girls are five and three at the time.

There is a teacher that lives in the apartment underneath ours. Every day the building manager is knocking on my door stating this teacher has complained about the noise of the girls running on the floor.

I try to tell him that if they had wings, they could fly but they don't. He understands. He hates coming to my apartment but says he has to because of her complaint. She is relentless downstairs My girls are typical toddlers. They run from the living room to kitchen etc. If they're watching TV and there's a commercial on, of course they're going to run fast to the bathroom and back. She complains still.

Gaynor is ready to start kindergarten. I register her and off we go with Julie in tow to take her to school. I cry my eyes out dropping her off. She is only there for half a day.

I get a call one day to come and pick her up early, the school is being evacuated. I head down to the school and find out that there is a moose running around on the school grounds, so for everyone's safety the school is closed for the rest of the day.

We spend our weekends going down to the beach. It isn't far from the apartment so we walk down there. A lot of families are there enjoying swimming also. It is on the Ottawa River. I then find out that Glynn is being transferred to Bruce Nuclear plant for a short time so we stay in Deep River for another year by ourselves. Glynn sends money every payday to me for the rent, bills, food etc. The call finally comes in that he will be working in a city called Ajax. He will start working in Pickering shortly. The company pays for our move, so the moving people come, pack our belongings and Glynn comes back to Deep and we are set to drive to Ajax.

My childhood years come back to me. The teacher that complains all the time, I decide to give her a little bit of payback. We are due to leave at 6am as it's a long trip to Ajax. We wake around 4 am. I let the girls run up and down the floors and skip with their skipping ropes at for at least an hour before we leave.

I never have to see this teacher downstairs again. I feel great that I can actually give back to a teacher what was given to me. It feels good. Off we go.

Chapter 16
Moving to Ajax

Five hours later we arrive at our new home in Ajax. It is about 30 minutes from Toronto. Glynn starts on the Monday at Pickering.

I register Gaynor and Julie for school at Lord Elgin. I find work not long after that at a company called Surefit. They make covers to go over couches, chairs, and loveseats.

There are a lot of brits that work there. We soon all hook up and hang out going to a British club on the weekends and have BBQ's at each other's houses. Glynn and I especially like a guy named Art Jones and his wife. Art works with me at Surefit.

We end up living there for four years and then Glynn gets offered another job back in Brantford. Off we go again. He ends up working at several companies in Brantford. Millwrights are in big demand so if he doesn't like one job, he can quit on a Friday and start another new job on Monday. We save all we can, and we take the girls back to England for Christmas or summer vacations.

I remember one particular Christmas and we were at Manchester airport. The girls got the two cutest stuffed donkeys from Father Christmas. In Manchester we pick up a trolley to check them in for baggage and they got the royal treatment. Everyone in the airport saw them being specially taken through to baggage by staff and were commenting how adorable these two donkeys were.

Our worse time was in Heathrow Airport in London. Glynn had to fly back to Canada a week before we did as he had to work. Our flight home was delayed. They give us a voucher to get food and drinks while we wait to board our airplane. Not one flight was leaving this day. We hear that there had been a drug bust in the morning so all flights are temporarily grounded while they do their investigation. I threw a fit in the airport cafeteria.

The girls are bored, tired, and hungry so we decide to go get some food and something to drink. I want a cup of tea so bad. I get in the line-up and lo and behold there are no clean teacups. I ask a worker if I can have a cup. He tells me that there are none clean, I will have to wait. My patience is gone by now. I'm sure you can imagine the tension and stress of probably 20,000 people all stuck in a small area with nothing to do for twelve hours. I ask him if he or someone else can wash some cups, only to be rudely told that it isn't his job. I scream and yell at him to go tell someone to do their damn job then, we all need a drink.

Finally we can sit down and have a cup of tea and something to eat. We all end up being stranded at the airport for twelve hours. We finally board our flight to Toronto and rather than arriving at 4pm, we are arriving at 4am instead.

All of the passengers on the flight are fed up. We just want to get home. The Captain announces that we are approaching Toronto. After this announcement everyone in the plane stands up, puts their hand over their heart and all you can hear is three hundred plus people singing, "Oh Canada," we are so glad to be home. It was amazing to see. I'm sure there is not another flight like this.

One year we take the girls to Florida. It is October so the girls will be missing a week of school. I inform the teacher of this. She tells me that is fine, the girls will learn more in a week there, than a week in a classroom. Gaynor's teacher assigns her to do a diary. At the end of the day Gaynor has to record every place we go to see. Florida is great. We go to Disney World of course, Kennedy Space Center, Busch Gardens, and go to the ocean.

I also bring my mum and my sister Brenda to Canada for a vacation as often as I can. One of those vacations we decide to rent a cottage in Rice Lake Ontario. We spend the week fishing. It is so much fun. Mum and Brenda have a great time. We barbeque and have a fire at night. Rice Lake is so pretty and peaceful.

I find another job at a sewing factory. I am hired to work in the cutting room as a cutter. The company makes sportswear. They make shirts and pants for baseball, hockey, soccer, and basketball. I stay there for about ten years then find another job at a different sports company still in the cutting room. I am still a cutter, but I also work in the shipping department when needed and do pattern making.

I work there for a few years. Jamie, the owner, decides to hire a manager called Roy. He is constantly coming into our department and telling us what we are doing is wrong. He has no experience, as far as I know, in the sewing industry but he likes to think he does. This goes on for probably a year or more. I am fed up by this point.

I march into his office one day and yell at him that I am sick of him trying to undermine our work and that we know what we're doing. I told him that we ran the cutting department quite well before him, and would do after too. He tried to apologize but I tell him I don't want an apology. Let us do our work. The next morning I get into work and there is a note on the board. It says Rose I'm sorry for everything. Roy. I marched into his office again and told him that I had said I did not want an apology. I then told him that at the end of the day, I won't be returning tomorrow. I quit then.

Glynn gets offered a new job signing up apprentices for the government. He loves that job. His area is Hamilton. He spends his days driving to different companies to sign up apprentices. At night, he also gets hired as a part-time teacher at Mohawk College and stays there for about ten years. I still work at the sewing factory.

Chapter 17
Deaths in the Family

I lose my beloved mum Christmas Eve of 1981. Louisa passes away December 24, 1981. I am devastated. I get on a plane and fly home for the funeral. She was my rock; I will forever miss her.

Glynn has to work so I meet up with my sister Jean in Toronto airport. Jean and George moved to Alberta in 1977. We fly to England together and are there for three weeks.

The same year my sister Brenda passes. She is only thirty-five. She is way too young to be gone. Gaynor and I fly home for her funeral. Again we meet up with Jean in Toronto and we all head home. The three of us end up there for three weeks. The funeral isn't going to happen for ten days because of the offices being closed for New Years; and she has to have an autopsy. There's lots of paperwork and just general mourning.

Glynn is very popular as a teacher and soon gets offered a full-time job as a teacher in a town near where we used to live in Ajax called Whitby. He works for Durham College teaching the millwrights. He loves opening the minds of young men and teaching in general

Whitby is two and a half hours from Brantford so Glynn and I decide it will be better for him if he moves to Whitby and rents an apartment during the week. The girls and I and their husbands help pack up his belongings and we move him to Whitby. He has rented a small apartment.

To pass those lonely nights I love to sew and knit. I make outfits for my grandkids for Christmas, I make pajama sets for a handicapped home here in Brantford. I drop them off a couple of days before Christmas wrapped up so the clients have something to open Christmas day and new clothing to wear. Gardening is a passion of mine, as well as cake decorating. I keep myself busy.

Glynn is very popular with his students. He stays after hours to help them if they are confused. I take the bus to Whitby when I can and spend the weekends with him, or he drives home. It is so hard being away from him but I know he loves his job so I put up with the distance. Glynn has some medical issues but he still keeps teaching. I am very worried about him. He has about five more years until he can retire.

Unfortunately, his health takes a turn for the worse and he is forced to leave. He comes back home to Brantford. We have three grandchildren. They are David, Nick, and Abby. Glynn is not happy that he cannot work. We end up selling the house we are in and buy a smaller house.

As we are getting ready to move Glynn falls ill and ends up in the hospital. The kids and I are forced to do all the packing and move ourselves. Glynn is hospitalized for two months.

We finally end up at the new house and are happy for about a year. Glynn is getting sicker and sicker. He is in and out of the hospital for the next year. Glynn ends up falling and passing out and is hospitalized January 3rd. His health is declining. He goes in with pneumonia. Week by week he is declining. He is losing his ability to move, then the ability to talk. I sit by him the last month. I hardly ever leave his bedside.

I feed him and talk to him, but he is no longer there. Ten days before he passes we are told he has stage four- cancer. From that day I never leave his side.

My youngest daughter Julie stays with me the night before he passes. We know it will only be a matter of hours now. We are woken up at 12:12 am by a big bang we hear in the room. Julie goes over to Glynn's bed, and he is gone. I call Gaynor and she races up to the hospital. The rest of the family follows after her. My beloved Glynn is gone. It is April 3, 2018.

Life goes on and I am now 75. We are married 55 ½ years. I feel like a part of my heart is gone. Thank goodness my girls are there to look after me.

Gaynor asks me how the abuse has affected me in my adult life. Well I will say this. I still do not know how to swim. It is too late to learn now.

The relatives come over from England for a visit. We take them to a park, and they all go in the pool. Gaynor's son David has a cramp and starts going under.

My sister Jean and I are the closest to him, so I let instinct and fear take over, I run in the pool and pull him up and out to safety. I probably could have drowned too, but my thoughts were to get him. He was pulled out and was fine.

I am sure you are all wondering how years of child abuse has affected me in life. Well here is how it has affected me in some way.

I do not like males bossing me around. I shut down or get very angry in return. I have had co-workers that want to boss me around and I put them in their place. One in particular, Dave, is an East Indian co-worker who calls me vile names. I burst out crying. My three co-workers are male. I tell my boss, Tom, what happens, but he takes it with a grain of salt and does nothing. I call Gaynor that night and she knows something is wrong. I explain what Dave has said to me at work.

Gaynor is livid. She is working for a police force at this time and talks to an officer. He in turn files a report, then goes over to this gentleman's home, if you can call him a gentleman. I certainly don't.

Dave is told if he ever uses that language to me again, he will be charged. I am 60 plus years at this time, I do not appreciate being called vile names and shown no respect.

He is in his 40s, married with two sons of his own. After this I go back to work for the money only, I certainly don't like the work environment or have any respect for my boss after this.

I give people a couple of chances and if they wrong me, that's it I'm done. I will not be put on by anyone. Never again will I allow anyone to do that to me. If someone does something to me, I don't like; I stay away from them, and shut them out of my life.

I get very angry when I hear of criminals in court complaining that they grew up in an abused home and it led them to a life of crime. I lived through abuse and had a great life. I find that a sorry excuse.

To this day I still cannot eat celery. It takes me back to that boiled celery in the school canteens. If I have a salad and see celery, I don't eat it. I said to Gaynor the other day how much I love going to thrift stores. It seems because I grew up with hand-me-downs that

I prefer that. I hate seeing anything wasted, whether it be clothes or food. I grew up with hardly any food due to the war. I was tough on my girls growing up if they left food on their plates. I do not like throwing food away that could and should be eaten.

I do try to help the Red Cross and the Salvation Army whenever I can because they helped my family and me out so much as kids. If it wasn't for either of these Organizations, I don't know where we would be.

Yes, abuse affects children. You can turn it around, or let it swallow you and you spend your life full of hate. Or you can change your outlook. I chose to rise above it. I am not that intimidated, scared little girl anymore that cowered. I don't trust a lot of people. I am very guarded. I don't easily share my feelings and I have a small circle of friends who I completely trust. It isn't easy to make friends with me; I am very guarded after my early years.

I suppose it has had a very big impact on my life, but I try not to let it rule me. I am grateful for all the good things I have.

My last words about child abuse is: One thing I have learned after my abuse as a child is, anybody with nicer clothes, might look nice on the outside, but it does not make them a better person. Beauty is truly only skin deep.

I do not like being called names, and I don't like anyone mad at me.

Chapter 18
The Final Wrap Up

Mom and I took our time getting all the information for this. She had gone through two surgeries on her eyes and a broken wrist. I didn't want to overwhelm her. I did tell mom about this and I would only write it if she gave me her blessing. She did. We spent endless hours laughing over things, and I could see the abuse part she was bothered by it, but also knew that it had happened, there was nothing she could do now, couldn't do then so she has accepted it. If she forgot to tell me something she would call me, tell me what it was and hang up. I did the same things also.

She cannot get any information from her siblings as most of them have died. Out of the eight kids, there is only three alive, her, my Auntie Jean (who lives on the other side of the country), and her elder sister Ellen who still lives in St. Helen's. While growing up if any of the siblings was abused, they never told her about it. She only remembers Aunty Jean once telling her about the losing the needle story.

This is a famous Liverpool song that breaks my heart every time I listen to it, as it was being played as the love of my life Glynn was passing. My grandson David played it in the room.

For Glynn,
The Love of My Life

You'll Never Walk Alone

When you walk through a storm
Hold your head up high
And don't be afraid of the dark
At the end of a storm
There's a golden sky
And the sweet silver song of a lark
Walk on through the wind
Walk on through the rain
Though your dreams be tossed and blown

Walk on, walk on
With hope in your heart
And you'll never walk alone
You'll never walk alone
Walk on, walk on
With hope in your heart
And you'll never walk alone
You'll never walk alone

This song is from Gerry and the Pacemakers, Liverpool

Glynn you never will walk alone, not as long as we're around. We love and miss you every single day.

English Terms

Butty – Sandwich
Fortnight –Two weeks
Jelly – Jell-O
Bangers and Mash –Sausage and Mashed potatoes
Sweets – Candy
Colliery – Coal mine
Windscreen – Windshield
Football – Soccer

Author Gaynor Jones is a married, mother of two children, who graduated in 2018 with honours from a Law Clerk program. She has written a non-fiction memoir about her mother's abuse at school in England due to Rose being poor. The title is Rose's Tale: The Strap, The Wooden Compass, The Endless Abuse at School.

Her mother Rose's health has deteriorated, so Gaynor wants the world to know the abuse children suffered through while growing up in England in the 1940s and 1950s by their teachers.

Gaynor has diplomas as a Law Clerk, and an Office Administrator Executive Secretary where she worked for years through her provincial government. Her hobbies include cooking, baking, gardening. Her interests include playing with her two guinea pigs, Reese, and Marble.

The Author was born near Liverpool, England and came to Canada as a young girl settling in Brantford, Ontario. Her passion has always been writing. During her school years she excelled in writing class. She is passionate about telling stories that have never been told before. Gaynor has also finished writing a book based on her daughter Abigail (Abby). Abby has been an air cadet from the ages of 12-18 years. Gaynor is hoping that those youth under 12-years-old will be interested in her book, love what the air cadets have to offer, and join. The story is called Gabby's Journey-The Making of a Canadian Air Cadet Pilot.

Gaynor was a book nerd growing up. Her favourite books were the *Nancy Drew* and *Hardy Boys* series. Even in high school, Gaynor's nose would always be in a book.

CPSIA information can be obtained
at www.ICGtesting.com
Printed in the USA
LVHW051055300321
682940LV00004B/313